MALE AND FEMALE, ONE IN CHRIST

D1021647

MALE *and* FEMALE ONE *in* CHRIST

New Testament Teaching on Women in Office

Clarence Boomsma

BAKER BOOK HOUSE
Grand Rapids, Michigan 49516

© 1993 by Clarence Boomsma

Published by Baker Books
a division of Baker Book House Company
P.O. Box 6287, Grand Rapids, MI 49516-6287

Second printing, January 1994

Printed in the United States of America

All rights reserved. No part of this publication may be reproduced, stored in a retrieval system, or transmitted in any form or by any means—electronic, mechanical, photocopy, recording, or any other—without the prior written permission of the publisher. The only exception is brief quotations in printed reviews.

Library of Congress Cataloging-in-Publication Data

Boomsma, Clarence.
    Male and female, one in Christ : New Testament teaching on women in office / Clarence Boomsma.
        p.   cm.
    ISBN 0-8010-1067-5
    1. Women in the Bible. 2. Women in Christianity—Biblical teaching. 3. Women in Christianity—History—Early church, ca. 30–600. 4. Bible. N.T.—Criticism, interpretation, etc. 5. Ordination of women—Biblical teaching. 6. Ordination of women—Christian Reformed Church. 7. Christian Reformed Church—Doctrines. 8. Reformed Church—Doctrines. I. Title.
    BS2545.W65B66   1993
    262'.14'082—dc20   93-14845

Unless noted otherwise, all Scripture quotations are taken from the HOLY BIBLE: NEW INTERNATIONAL VERSION®. NIV®. Copyright © 1973, 1978, 1984 by International Bible Society. Used by permission of Zondervan Publishing House. Other versions cited are the Authorized Version (AV), the Jerusalem Bible (JB), and the Revised Standard Version (RSV).

To **Shirley**
wife and life-partner
companion and friend

Contents

Preface

The literature on the role of women in the leadership of the church is enormous. In writing this book I confined the subject matter primarily to the issue as it has been expressed in the Christian Reformed Church in North America. I have not attempted to discuss every argument and detail that have surfaced, lest the book become too long and involved to serve its purpose. I have tried to focus on the heart of the matter by addressing the primary biblical data around which the debate centers. I believe the contention on women in office in my denomination is a paradigm of what is happening in other churches. As such I hope this book may have some value for the wider audience of conservative and evangelical churches.

I am indebted to Richard Baker, president of Baker Book House, who offered to publish this book, when I first approached him for advice on how to proceed to have the book published privately. He expressed his desire to be its publisher, saying that he knew how his father, the late Herman Baker, founder of the firm and my friend of many years, had wished I would walk into his office one day with a manuscript for publication. Richard introduced me to

Maria den Boer, whose editorial skills and warm encouragement have been so helpful.

I must express my appreciation to friends and colleagues who urged me to write the book and offered profitable suggestions, among them the Rev. Tymen E. Hofman, who first suggested and pressed me to write the book. I must acknowledge my indebtedness to several whose expertise significantly improved the book, but who bear no responsibility for its weaknesses. President Dr. James De Jong of Calvin Theological Seminary and Dr. Bastiaan Van Elderen, recently retired professor of New Testament, offered insightful critiques. Dr. Cornelius Plantinga, professor of systematic theology and my valued friend, read and reread the manuscript during its composition, offering useful improvements and continued encouragement. Most of all I wish to express my deep appreciation to Dr. Henry Stob, retired professor of apologetics and ethics, my close and treasured friend for nearly fifty-five years, for his generous assistance and reassuring support. His acute and logical mind and his meticulous use of words have greatly improved this book. And not least I must thank my wife, Shirley, for her support and patience during the months of writing, when, as she says, she endured being a "WIO (Women in Office) widow."

Clarence Boomsma
March 18, 1993

Introduction: *A Church in Tension*

The issue of permitting women to serve as ministers and elders in the Christian Reformed Church in North America has become a seriously contentious and divisive controversy in the denomination. The decision of the Synod of 1990 that permitted "churches to use their discretion in utilizing the gifts of women members in all offices of the church" unleashed a storm of protests and threats of schism.

The propriety of women serving as deacons had already been settled in 1984 after six years of protracted debate. In 1990 the Synod, wearied by what appeared to be the inconclusive results after nearly twenty years of study, made its decision to permit congregations to decide for themselves whether to ordain women as ministers and elders. Synod, however, requested churches not to implement the decision of 1990 until the required church order changes were ratified in 1992. It also instructed the Board of Publications to prepare a booklet designed to provide the church with a concise summary of the synodical studies and actions that preceded the decision to permit the ordination of women. It was titled *Women in Office: A Report to the Christian Reformed Churches.*

A barrage of articles and several pamphlets appeared in reaction to the controversial action of the Synod of 1990. *The Banner* carried a few articles on both sides of the question. Dr. John W. Cooper, professor of philosophical theology, wrote a white paper, *A Cause for Division?* subtitled *Women in Office and the Unity of the Church*. It was "prepared in dialogue with the faculty of the Calvin Theological Seminary" and published by the seminary. But most of the literature came from opponents of the decision, all of it arguing for the reversal of the 1990 decision. The conservative press, including *The Outlook* and *Christian Renewal*, launched and continued a strong protest. Two members of the faculty of Mid-America Reformed Seminary published *A Cause of Division*, subtitled *The Hermeneutic of Women's Ordination*, in critical response to Dr. Cooper's booklet. New publications appeared, groups were organized, rallies were held, and meetings were called to consider and even prepare for separation from the church.

The 1991 Synod received numerous overtures and protests against the decision of 1990, primarily on the basis that no biblical grounds had been provided to justify the radical departure from the longstanding position and practice of the church. The Synod of 1991, therefore, decided "to appoint a small ad hoc committee to gather from the various synodical study committee reports and related publications the biblical grounds for the decision" (*Acts of Synod 1991*, p. 729).

In November 1991, meeting the date requested by Synod, the ad hoc committee submitted its report, including four summarizing statements to serve as grounds for the decision of the Synod of 1990. Two copies were sent to each church. The intention of Synod that it should be made "available before the winter of 1991–1992 season of study" to "further facilitate the pastoral and reflective process envisioned by Synod 1990" was not realized (*Acts of Synod 1991*, p. 730). It appeared as Report 31 in the *Agenda for Synod 1992* (pp. 359–83). Critical responses to the report began to appear in the conservative press in the spring of 1992 and the editor of *The Banner* took appreciative note of it shortly before Synod met, but otherwise it received very little public exposure.

When the Synod of 1992 assembled it soon became evident that the body was more concerned about trying to keep the church together than seeking to ascertain the biblical basis for or against women in the offices of the church.

When the Synod of 1992 assembled it soon became evident that the body was more concerned about trying to keep the church together than seeking to ascertain the biblical basis for or against women in the offices of the church. As a result, Report 31 appeared to have little interest for the delegates. The majority of the advisory committee gave it only a cursory glance and recommended that the decision of 1990 not be ratified, stating merely "that the biblical support for ordination presented in Report 31 is not sufficiently persuasive to win the confidence and support of the church," as if the report had been widely studied and evaluated (*Acts of Synod 1992*, p. 699). Nor did the committee even begin to demonstrate why the exegesis and argumentation of the report were not persuasive. There were numerous overtures before Synod that took issue with Report 31, but the ad hoc committee had no opportunity to enter into serious discussion about the criticisms. Their meeting with the members of the advisory committee was little more than a perfunctory courtesy.

Synod itself, as the editor of *The Banner* wrote, "barely sniffed at the statements and then went on" (*The Banner*, June 29, 1992, p. 5). He wondered why the ad hoc committee had even bothered to prepare the report with its grounds. The real motivation of the Synod appeared in the second ground for the decision not to ratify the change in the church order: "There is reason to believe that ratification would aggravate the current unrest and divisiveness in the church, and therefore ratification would not be prudent in the current polarized situation" (*Acts of Synod 1992*, p. 699).

The majority of the advisory committee members struggled to find a compromise by which members on both sides of the issue could submit a unified report. A member of the committee later reported that they did not try to convince one another to change their positions. They simply asked what, in view of the wide diversity within the committee (which they assumed was reflective of the church), would be the best decision for Synod to make. They believed they achieved their goal by both sides compromising for the sake of the unity of the church. As a result, Synod not only failed to ratify the decision of 1990, but adopted an additional and amazing decision. It read: "Synod encourages the churches to use the gifts of women members to the fullest extent possible in their local churches, including allowing women to teach, expound the Word of God and provide pastoral care under the supervision of the elders" (*Acts of Synod 1992*, p. 700).

Apart from the fine sticking point of ordination that is required to preach the Word and administer the sacraments, the Synod opened the pulpits of Christian Reformed churches to women totally at the discretion of the elders. It is true they may not "preach" as ordained ministers, or "exhort" as licensed students. They may only "expound" the Word of God. Does this mean "expound" as Jesus expounded to the Emmaus Road travelers from "all the Scriptures the things concerning himself" (Luke 24:27 AV), and as Priscilla and Aquila took Apollos aside and "expounded to him the way of God more accurately" (Acts 18:26 RSV), and as the apostle Paul expounded the gospel to the leaders of the Jews in Rome during his imprisonment, trying "to convince them about Jesus" (Acts 28:23 RSV)?

It would seem women may now "preach" without the restrictions normally placed upon men when they occupy the pulpit, and without any supervision of Classis or Synod. The only safeguard is the elders, who are bound by their loyalty to the form of subscription when they authorize a woman to expound (explain, interpret) the Bible in sermonic form in a worship service.

The Synod of 1992 created ecclesiastical chaos. It is difficult to believe that anyone can be pleased with the present state of affairs. Thus, it appears inevitable that the whole matter will need to be addressed again by a following Synod, if not by the Synod of 1993.

The Synod of 1990 was widely criticized for not providing biblical grounds for its decision to permit churches to ordain women. The Synod of 1992 refused to ratify the 1990 decision, without any serious discussion of the biblical data and without providing biblical grounds. By merely citing textual references and Lord's Day 21 of the Heidelberg Catechism, it opened for all practical purposes the offices of minister and elder to women, restricted only by the supervision of male elders, a supervision that has always applied to men.

> *The Synod of 1992 refused to ratify the 1990 decision, without any serious discussion of the biblical data and without providing biblical grounds.*

I was one of the three members who served on the ad hoc committee. I accepted the appointment in part because I had never come to reasoned clarity on the question of women in office in light of a careful study of the Scriptures. I thought serving on this committee would require of me a careful listening to what the synodical study committees had written on the biblical data as well as an in-depth reading of the Bible. This has proved to be the case.

In view of the chaotic state of the question after the decisions of the Synod of 1992 and the almost inevitable return of the matter to the synodical agenda, I believe it may be of some use to share with others the fruits of my odyssey through the Scriptures as it bears on the role of women in the offices of the church. I have been encouraged and urged to do so. In this book I draw on the report of the ad hoc committee, and seek to take into account the criticism that was alleged against the report in synodical overtures and various publications. But that report was necessarily limited by the committee's mandate to gather and organize the data from the synodical study committee reports from 1972 to 1990 and related publications. This book contains additional material as a result of my study and reflection on the biblical data. I am indebted to many sources, but no attempt is made to acknowledge them, except in a few instances.

I do not fault the advisory committee for seeking to promote the peace and to preserve the unity of the church. Its recommendation was a political move, but not without honest concern for a very fundamental truth of the gospel: the unity of the church for which Christ prayed so fervently on the eve of his crucifixion.

Its recommendation was a political move, but not without honest concern for a very fundamental truth of the gospel: the unity of the church for which Christ prayed so fervently on the eve of his crucifixion.

The issue of women in office is, however, a serious matter. On the one hand, the fundamental questions of biblical authority and interpretation cannot be ignored in the debate. On the other hand, unless it is clear that the teaching of the Scriptures requires such prohibition, to continue to bar women from the opportunity to exercise fully their gifts in the life of the church, including the substantial and influential roles of teaching and leadership, is to perpetuate an injustice against women and possibly be in disobedience to the Word of God.

My purpose is not to write another book to add to the many books about the role of women in the church, but to address the issue in the CRC from my perspective. Contrary to what is alleged by opponents of women in office, I, along with many others in the church, hold that an interpretation of the scriptural data that justifies the synodical decision of 1990 without calling into question the inspiration and infallibility of the Bible is possible.

This book is intended to help members of the Christian Reformed Church read the Scriptures and see that ordaining women as ministers and elders is permissible and even proper in the light of God's Word.

This book is intended to help members of the Christian Reformed Church read the Scriptures and see that ordaining women as ministers and elders is permissible and even proper in the light of God's Word.

I have come to see that Paul's prohibition against women believers teaching and exercising authority in the church is rooted not in a timeless principle of female subordination. Rather, as in the case of slavery, it is based on the timeless principle of not fostering unnecessary offense that would hinder the furtherance of the gospel by going against prevailing social conventions.

1

The Controversy's
New Testament Roots

How did we come to have the issue of women in office that is so controversial and divisive in the Christian Reformed Church?

The immediate occasion is the attempt to expand equal opportunities for women in political, legal, and economic status, in the areas of education, employment, and marriage, and in the freedom to compete with men in all areas of life, which began in the mid-nineteenth century and has continued until the present. In 1920, after years of debate and agitation, the Nineteenth Amendment to the Constitution of the United States legalized woman suffrage. At the time the CRC officially decided that the issue was not an ecclesiastical matter; therefore, Synod did not take a position on the question of women's rights in society. The issue did, however, occasion considerable negative discussion in the church and its press at the time. In

1947 the question of whether women could vote at congregational meetings first appeared on the synodical agenda. In 1957 it was finally approved as an option for consistories. A few churches still do not permit women to vote in congregational meetings.

Meanwhile, in the post–World War II era and particularly in the revolutionary 1960s the role of women in church life aroused much discussion. The majority of churches, such as the Roman Catholic Church, the Orthodox churches, the large Southern Baptist and Missouri Synod Lutheran churches, and many conservative and evangelical denominations do not permit women to occupy positions of authority. In the 1980s and 1990s there developed a widespread acceptance of women serving in the ecclesiastical offices in the so-called mainline Protestant churches in Europe and North America and also among evangelical denominations, some of whom are members of the National Association of Evangelicals.

The question of women occupying the ecclesiastical offices of the church arose historically in the Christian Reformed Church when the Reformed Ecumenical Synod (now Council) asked its member churches in 1970 to study its report on women in office. In response, Synod appointed what proved to be the first of a series of committees to study the teachings of Scripture on the position of women in the life of the church.

While broad social changes may be the occasion for the modern question of women in office, it is important to realize that the roots of the issue in the church today are embedded in the history of the Christian church from its beginning. That the function of women in positions of leadership was already a serious dispute in the early church is evident in the New Testament. Only the existence of this controversial issue can explain the presence of such passages as 1 Corinthians 11:3–16 and 14:33–36, and 1 Timothy 2:11–15. In these texts Paul addresses the dissension in the churches of Corinth and Ephesus regarding the status of women in the congregations, instructions that today are the subject of so much exegetical study and debate in the CRC.

> *While broad social changes may be the occasion for the modern question of women in office, it is important to realize that the roots of the issue in the church today are embedded in the history of the Christian church from its beginning.*

What is the background to these controversies? Even a cursory reading of the New Testament in comparison with the Old Testament makes it unmistakably clear that something happened to give women a higher status in the church. In Judaism, according to Josephus, a woman was "in every respect of less worth than a man." In the temple a woman was allowed to go only as far as the Court of the Women. From the religious perspective she was on the same level as a slave. She did not have to pray the "Shema" morning and evening because she was not mistress of her own time. Women were kept in seclusion to safeguard morality; if they left their homes they wore veils.

But in the sphere of the kingdom proclaimed by Jesus as reported in the Gospel accounts a fundamentally different attitude toward women appears. That the writers included these accounts in the Gospels is itself a noteworthy testimony to the change effected by the coming of Christ. In the kingdom, there is no devaluation of women. Jesus dissociates himself from the rigid practice of keeping women in seclusion.

> *That the writers included these accounts in the Gospels is itself a noteworthy testimony to the change effected by the coming of Christ.*

People of Jesus' day sought to protect women by secluding them, believing that the sexual desire of males was nearly uncontrollable. Jesus accepted women into his group of followers because he expected his disciples to control their desires. In Matthew 5:28 Jesus teaches that purity must rule; even a man's gaze must be disciplined. "Do not speak much with a woman (on the street)," says an old rabbinic proverb, but Jesus talks openly with a woman from Samaria, to the amazement of his disciples (John 4:4–42).

It is an interesting aside, that, when in Luke 23:2 we read that the Jews accused Jesus before Pilate of perverting the people, a textual variant adds "and perverting the women and the children." This variant suggests that there was an early awareness of the revolutionary character of Jesus' acceptance of women. In contrast to Old Testament practices, in the New Testament women are active participants and occupy a significant place in society. Women have a new status, a new recognition, and a new opportunity for service.

In contrast to Old Testament practices, in the New Testament women are active participants and occupy a significant place in society.

It is clear from the Gospels that the change in the position of and respect for women was the direct result of Jesus' teaching about the coming of the kingdom of God as well as his own practice. Ordinarily women were identified by the name of their husbands, but the women who follow Jesus are called by name in the Gospels. Mary Magdalene, Joanna, Susanna, and many others who were helping support Jesus and the disciples out of their own means (Luke 8:2–3) probably became persons of prominence in the New Testament church. Jesus, in marked contrast to Jewish customs, teaches the Samaritan woman at the well and she becomes his witness to her people (John 4:2–42). He befriends Mary and Martha (their brother Lazarus is mentioned only in reference to his death) and in utter disregard for the custom of the day commends Mary for her interest in his teaching (Luke 10:42). He bestows great prominence and honor on Mary, who anoints his body for burial (Matt. 26:13). He dialogues with the Syro-Phoenician woman, whose great faith he commends and whose daughter he heals (Matt. 15:28). In his parables Jesus gives significant recognition to women in illustrating the kingdom.

What is of particular and astonishing significance is the report in the Gospels that women are the first witnesses to the resurrection of Jesus. That in itself could be considered an accident of history, but that the risen Lord appeared to these women and commissioned them to testify to his disciples of his resurrection (Matt. 28:7, 10) was our Lord's deliberate intention. This is the more remarkable because the current view was that women along with slaves were not qualified to bear legal witness. Jesus rebukes the disciples for not believing Mary Magdalene's testimony (Mark 16:14; John 20:18). When addressing the question of women in office, serious consideration must be given to the astonishing fact that Jesus chose women to be the initial witnesses to the foundational event on which all Christian preaching is based!

Jesus chose women to be the initial witnesses to the foundational event on which all Christian preaching is based!

As in the Gospels, women receive notable prominence in the Acts of the Apostles. At Pentecost women along with men are given the signs and gifts of the Holy Spirit. They too receive the prophetic gift of the Holy Spirit in fulfillment of Joel's prophecy (2:28–32) that women and slaves as well as men would be the recipients of this gift in the age to come. This is especially meaningful because the biblical gift of prophecy is today equated with preaching in Reformed thinking (cf. *Acts of Synod 1973*, pp. 450–53). Women along with men are persecuted for their testimony (Acts 8:3). Dorcas is singled out as a "disciple" engaged in deeds of mercy (Acts 9:36). That the four daughters of Philip are explicitly mentioned as possessing the gift of prophecy emphasizes their role in the early church (Acts 21:9).

In 1 Corinthians 12:28 we read that in the church God has appointed first apostles, second prophets, third teachers. Those who prophesy are ranked just below the apostles and above teachers in the hierarchy of church leadership. In the New Testament women, as well as men, are gifted to serve as prophets. It is reasonable to suppose that women could serve as well in the lesser role of official teachers in the church.

Women play an important part in the ministry of the apostle Paul as is evident from the Book of Acts and his epistles. They help him establish churches and maintain their life and witness. Lydia, the affluent merchant, is Paul's first convert in Europe, and she opens her home to him and apparently to the Philippian congregation (Acts 16:14–15). Priscilla and her husband Aquila (she is named first five out of the seven times they are mentioned in the New Testament) instruct the evangelist, Apollos, and help him understand the gospel more clearly (Acts 18:26). Paul speaks of Euodia and Syntyche along with Clement (a man) as his fellow workers who "contended at my side in the cause of the gospel" (Phil. 4:2–3). He notes the outstanding service of Phoebe as a deaconess to the church in Cenchreae (Rom. 16:1–2). It is remarkable that the apostle greets by name no less than seven women in Romans 16. These women were undoubtedly strong and notable leaders in the church of Rome.

It is against this background of the revolutionary change in the attitude toward women in the New Testament church, initiated by the life and example of Jesus, confirmed in the outpouring of the Holy Spirit, and practiced in the early church Paul would have known, as well as the contribution women made in his own ministry, that we must read Paul's classic text in Galatians 3:28. In this momentous statement he proclaims the great truth of the equality of all believers in their oneness in Christ: "There is neither Jew nor Greek, slave nor free, male nor female, for you are all one in Christ Jesus." Joachim Jeremias states that this background is "the only possible explanation of the maxim in Gal. 3:28, that in Christ Jesus there is no difference between male and female, which is quite extraordinary for one who was born a Jew" (*New Testament Theology: The Proclamation of Jesus*, p. 27). It was the divine revelation of this dramatic change in the status of women in the life of the church that was used by the Holy Spirit to inspire the great apostle to pen these stupendous words.

Galatians 3:28 does not stand by itself, but embodies the entire New Testament teaching on women.

It is therefore quite wrong for opponents of women in office to say that the whole case for those who favor permitting women to serve in the offices hangs on only what may be implicit in one text, as if Galatians 3:28 were an isolated reference in the New Testament. The text does not stand by itself, but embodies the entire New Testament teaching on women.

Yet it is also the apostle Paul whose teachings in 1 Corinthians 11 and 14 and 1 Timothy 2 (the most important texts) place restrictions on the leadership of women in the life and practice of the early church. He did so apparently in response to the dissension and controversies that arose in the congregations out of the changed attitude toward and among women in the light of the gospel. As Professor F. W. Grosheide remarks: "the apostle fights on two fronts. On the one side it was necessary to put the emancipated Corinthian ladies in their places, but on the other Paul seeks to prevent the woman from being considered inferior" (Commentary on the First Epistle to the Corinthians, in *The New International Commentary on the New Testament*, p. 258).

Thus, there are two lines of thought in the New Testament. On the one hand, there is the testimony of the Gospels, the history of the New Testament church, and the theological teaching of unity and equality in Christ as expressed in Galatians 3:28, which appear to affirm the full equality of women to exercise their gifts in the life of the church. Only the presence of this line of thought in the fledgling church can account for women pressing for equality in the community of believers. On the other hand, there is the restraining line of Paul's explicit prohibitions restricting women from authoritative areas of the church's life, teaching them to be subservient to men.

The controversy in the New Testament church regarding the leadership roles of women arose out of the tension between these two lines of thought: the equality of women in Christ and their subservience under the headship of men. The controversy in the CRC regarding women in office stems from the interpretation of these two lines of thought in the New Testament and how they are to be applied to the church today.

> *The controversy in the New Testament church regarding the leadership roles of women arose out of the tension between these two lines of thought: the equality of women in Christ and their subservience under the headship of men.*

Perhaps it is well to state as precisely as we can at this point what it is at the heart of the issue that gives rise to the two contending views in the CRC on women in office.

It is not a question of whether women may use their gifts in the life of the church, including teaching and pastoral service. The question is whether they may serve as official teachers and ruling authorities. The heart of the issue is whether women may serve in the office of elders, whereby they rule over the church (Heb. 13:17) and therefore over males, and whether they may serve as pastors, that is, officially ordained teaching elders, who authoritatively teach members of the church, including males.

It is not a question of accepting the infallibility of the Word of God, but of the proper interpretation of the inspired Scriptures. Leading opponents charge that to favor women in office is to employ methods of biblical interpretation that are incompatible with humble submission to God's Word and a denial of its authority and full teaching. I am persuaded that the allegation is not true, and so we turn to the biblical data.

It is not a question of accepting the infallibility of the Word of God, but of the proper interpretation of the inspired Scriptures.

2

The Implications of Galatians 3:28

When the ad hoc committee began its study of the synodical reports on women in office, it soon concluded that Galatians 3:28 deserved more attention than had been given to it. Nearly all the reports agreed that the text spoke about the equality of Jews and Gentiles, slaves and freemen, males and females in their spiritual oneness in Christ, but also that this unity in Christ and equality before God had social implications for the life of the church.

This interpretation is the consensus of all competent commentators. Herman Ridderbos, in his 1953 commentary on Galatians, writing of the gulf between Jew and Greek spoke in addition of

> the tremendous separation which social inequality and the differentiation of sexes brought with them in ancient times. True, it is the religious contrast that is the bone of contention between Paul and his opponents, but the oneness

of master and slave, too, and the oneness of man and woman, in Christ, illustrates how completely the bond with Christ conquers all things and established them. . . . This is not to maintain that the natural and social distinction is in no respect relevant any more. . . . From the point of view of redemption in Christ, however, and of the gifts of the Spirit granted by Him, there is no preference of Jew to Greek, master to slave, man to woman. This has social consequences, too, although the apostle does not enter further upon them at this point. (p. 149)

William Hendricksen in his *New Testament Commentary* on *Galatians* comments:

What Paul is saying, then, is that all such distinctions—be they racial-religious ("neither Jew nor Greek"), social ("neither slave nor freeman"), or sexual ("no male and female")—must be thoroughly abandoned, since in Christ all are equal. . . . For a Jew to confess himself to be a Christian, and then to refuse to eat with Christians from the Gentiles, or to regard himself as being in any way superior to them in moral worth is an abomination to the Lord. Similarly today the church cannot tolerate hurtful distinctions. All believers are in a sense one person, one body "in Christ." . . . Christianity cannot tolerate any actions or decisions which because of race, social standing, or sex, would degrade certain individuals to the status of second-rate citizenship in the kingdom of heaven, or would even exclude them entirely from such citizenship. (pp. 150–51)

Even George W. Knight III, a strong opponent of women in office, says in his *The New Testament Teaching on the Role Relationship of Men and Women*: "Faith in Christ and nothing else brings one into spiritual unity with Christ *and into equality (cf. I Cor. 12) with all who are Christ's*" (p. 19; emphasis added). In fact, whenever reconciliation with God is experienced through Christ, it immediately and inevitably follows that there is reconciliation to life and reconciliation to other believers. Justification and sanctification are inseparable. To have the living Lord within means to relate to others as Christ would feel about them.

It is evident that Galatians 3:28 has social implications, but it does not address and thus does not answer whether it is proper for women to serve in the offices of the church. But its teaching on their equality in Christ and with all believers does raise the question about on what grounds women should be prohibited from serving in these offices. This crucial text requires careful consideration.

> *Its teaching on their equality in Christ and with all believers does raise the question about on what grounds women should be prohibited from serving in these offices.*

Paul's letter to the Galatian churches was written in response to the presence of so-called Judaizers who had come among them. These Jewish Christians taught that Gentiles, in addition to their simple belief in Christ, had to supplement their faith by circumcision and the observance of the Law of Moses in order to inherit salvation. The apostle strenuously opposes this teaching. He argues that salvation has always been through faith as was true for Abraham, the father of all believers (3:6–7). Therefore, whatever the role of the Law, it is through faith in Christ, apart from the works of the Law, that believers become the children of God (3:26).

In verse 27 Paul writes that the seal of faith is baptism (which has replaced circumcision) by which all believers are incorporated into the body of Christ, his church. The believer, in submitting to baptism, becomes Christ's person. He has "clothed himself with Christ" so that he is identified with Christ as a "new man." In verse 29 Paul concludes, "if you belong to Christ, then you are Abraham's seed, and heirs according to the promise."

It is the sweep of Paul's thought of believers being accepted as children of God (v. 26) that carries Paul beyond the question of circumcision and uncircumcision (6:15) to include slaves and women.

Galatians 3:28 is not essential to the flow of the argument Paul is developing in this passage. It is a digressive statement that can be omitted without any break in thought. There is no connective word, such as "since," "for," or "therefore," to demand that it be closely joined in thought to any specific element of what immediately precedes. It does not mean that there is no relation between verse 28 and verse 27, nor its setting in the pericope. Verse 28 stands in apposition to verse 27, thereby supplementing the thought of verse 27. It is the sweep of Paul's thought of believers being accepted as children of God (v. 26) that carries Paul beyond the question of circumcision and uncircumcision (6:15) to include slaves and women. Slaves and women are not in Paul's purview in this epistle, but he is inspired by the grandeur of the transformation and oneness of believers in Christ to see the vision of a fragmented humanity united by salvation in Christ. It is this view that rouses Paul to affirm that the discriminating distinctions of nationality, social status, and gender are abolished: "There is neither Jew nor Greek, slave nor free, male nor female, for you are all one in Christ Jesus."

In verse 28 Paul is saying more than that Jews and Greeks, slaves and freemen, males and females are all one in their vertical relationship with God through Christ, true as it is. By speaking of the baptism of believers and their imitation of Christ (having clothed themselves with Christ) in verse 27, the apostle has introduced the horizontal dimension of their being "in Christ." He is saying that, because they are united in Christ and have put on Christ, their relationships with one another are changed. Being members of the body of Christ, as signified in their baptism, they are no longer first of all Jew or Greek, slave or free, male and female to each other, but are all equally children of God.

It is on the basis of their unity in Christ that an equality exists that was not present outside Christ Jesus—an equality that has priority over the distinctions that made for their inequality apart from Christ. The basis for Galatians 3:28 is the vertical relationship between God and the believer taught in verses 26–27. The primary focus of verse 28 is the horizontal relationships of the Christian community that come into being because of the salvation sealed in baptism. As circumcision of only males in the Old Testament dispensation had profound social consequences in the Jewish society, so baptism that included females necessarily had profound meaning for the place and role of women in the church. Gilbert Bilezikian in *Beyond Sex Roles* states it well when he writes that "Galatians 3:28 does not describe the 'basis of membership in the body of Christ' . . . or the conditions for entering the church. It describes the conditions that should prevail within the body of Christ" (p. 277).

> *The primary focus of verse 28 is the horizontal relationships of the Christian community that come into being because of the salvation sealed in baptism.*

Opponents of women in office misread the text when they insist that it teaches only the vertical dimension—oneness in Christ with respect to salvation—and they err when they insist that equating this oneness in Christ with equality in Christ is unwarranted. They like to point out when Paul says, "for you are all one in Christ Jesus" he uses the Greek word *hen* for "one" and not the Greek word *isos* that means "equal," which he could have used if that was what he wanted to say, "for you are all equal in Christ Jesus." What the critics ignore is that in the construction of the sentence the element of equality is stressed by the triple use of *ouk eni*, which is translated "there is not." The text literally reads: "There is not Jew nor Greek, there is not freeman nor slave, there is not male and female, for you are all one in Christ Jesus." The various translations of *ouk eni* highlight the removal of inequality. The Authorized Version translates it, "There is neither"; Goodspeed and Moffatt, "There is no room for"; the Jerusalem Bible, "there are no more distinctions"; the New English Bible, "There is no such thing as"; the New Revised Standard Version, "There is no longer"; and Weymouth, "There cannot be." It would be faithful to the text to paraphrase it: "Jews and Greeks are now equal, slaves and freemen are now equal, males and females are now equal, for you are all one in Christ Jesus." So understood it is quite proper for Paul to have used *hen* ("one"), for it is the unity (oneness) in Christ that is the basis for the *ouk eni.*

To limit the interpretation of Galatians 3:28 to the spiritual relationship between the believer and God is to render the text redundant. The salvation of Jews and Gentiles, slaves and free, men and women was not in question when Paul wrote Galatians. In as far as it may ever have been in doubt, the life, teaching, and practice of Jesus, the Pentecost event, and Peter's experience with Cornelius would have settled that matter years before. Paul's ministry from the beginning was marked by the inclusion of all in the churches he established. To suggest that the text is only affirming that slaves can be saved without becoming freemen and that there was a current assumption that salvation was only for men is without any foundation. No, Paul is not belaboring the obvious in Galatians 3:28. Even an opponent has written: "No other verse of Scripture comes closer than this one to being a proof text for revising the historic position of the professing church to allow for the ordination of women" (Norman Shepherd, *Women in the Service of Christ*, p. 27). It comes much closer than opponents care to admit.

This unity and equality in the church, as we noted above, was the new environment that Paul experienced when he became a Christian. His inclusion of slaves and women is reminiscent of Peter's quote from Joel 2:28–32 on Pentecost that signaled the unity and equality of all believers in the outpouring of the Holy Spirit. Having received the Holy

Spirit and having clothed themselves with Jesus Christ they are all equally members of his body and participants in his mission to the world.

Paul is not saying that natural and social distinctions are abolished and no longer extant, but he is affirming that within the body of Christ the alienating and divisive effects of sin associated with the distinctions of nationality, social status, and gender are erased for those who are in Christ. When persons identify with Christ by faith, their spiritual allegiances take precedence over their racial or ethnic identifications, their social or legal classifications, and their gender distinctions as defined in our fallen world.

These distinctions remain but are immaterial to equality in the life of the church. The equality of people's potential for worth, function, responsibility, and authority lies in their unity with Christ, which is not restricted by their ethnicity, social status, or gender. Of course, equality does not mean that the capacities of all are the same, that all are biologically alike, that there are no dissimilarities in character and personality, in intellectual, emotional, and physical endowments, in spiritual gifts and talents. All such differences in individuals have a bearing on a person's suitability for particular service in the church as is taught in 1 Corinthians 12. But the point of Galatians 3:28 is that no person is unsuitable because of his or her nationality, social status, or gender. There is no room in the church for second-class members.

In 1 Corinthians 12:7–11 Paul speaks of various kinds of spiritual gifts and different types of service in the church. However, neither nationality, social status, nor gender have anything to do with the distinctions of gifts and functions.

In Colossians 3:7–11 the apostle describes how being in Christ revolutionizes his readers' behavior toward each other, including the removal of the discriminations common in the way they used to live: "Here there is no Greek or Jew, circumcised or uncircumcised, barbarian, Scythian, slave or free, but Christ is all and is in all."

> *The equality of people's potential for worth, function, responsibility, and authority lies in their unity with Christ, which is not restricted by their ethnicity, social status, or gender.*

Paul himself practiced the social implications of the theology he taught in Galatians 3:28. In Galatians 2:11–14 we learn that he opposed Peter for withdrawing from table fellowship with the Gentiles when the Judaizers were present. Paul knew that the spiritual fellowship in Christ between Jews and Greeks meant the renewal of their human and social relationships. Reading Paul's letters makes abundantly clear that he saw the social implications of the gospel of Galatians 3:28 in the relationships of slaves and masters (Col. 3:22–25) and between men and women (Eph. 5:21–33).

Women in the early church, having received the Holy Spirit and having been baptized into the church, recognized the significance of the gospel's teaching and sought to exercise their newfound liberty in the life of the congregation. Indeed, the women in Corinth and Ephesus may well have become so aggressive and abrasive in their demands for equality, that grasping for the prestige of teaching and leadership they caused serious dissension among the members in their congregations.

In 1 Corinthians 11:16 Paul makes reference to those who want to be contentious about the relations of men and women in the churches. This behavior is the only reasonable explanation for the familiar passages of 1 Corinthians 11 and 14 and 1 Timothy 2. They are Paul's response, in his time and circumstances, to the assertive behavior of women that was causing disruption and dissension in the congregations.

It is interesting that in 1 Corinthians 12:13, a parallel passage to Galatians 3:28, no mention is made of male and female. The absence is conspicuous. It is reasonable to suppose it was the special problem of dictatorial and usurping women in Corinth that prompted the apostle not to mention the inclusion of male and female as he does in Galatians 3:28.

It is understandable that Paul, out of concern for the progress of the gospel, did not advocate an assertive defense of women's liberty and their standing in the church in the male-dominated society of the Jews and Gentiles of his day. The assembly of the apostles and elders decided in deference to the strong social mores of the Jews to tell Gentiles to abstain from "the meat of strangled animals and from blood" (Acts 15:20) for the same reason. If the changes in the Jew-Gentile relations on circumcision nearly divided the churches, for Paul to have promoted this controversial issue might well have devastated the church. As in the case of slavery, the full implications of the inspired, redemption-based mandate of Galatians 3:28 had to await the Spirit's leading into a fuller understanding of the gospel of our liberty in Christ. There must always be room in the church for the process of growth in principles enunciated in the New Testament. The church must be open to the guidance of the Holy Spirit into a fuller understanding of the teachings of the gospel (John 14:26; 16:12–14).

The well-known and highly respected conservative theologian, J. I. Packer, although himself opposed to women serving as elders, writes that "the burden of proof regarding the exclusion of women from the office of teaching and ruling within the congregation now lies on those who maintain the exclusion rather than on those who challenge it" (*Women, Authority, and the Bible*, p. 298). In spite of the distinguished reputation of Dr. Packer, however, opponents caustically charge that such a "shifting of the burden of proof" is an unbecoming clever debating tactic and an "illegitimate ploy."

There must always be room in the church for the process of growth in principles enunciated in the New Testament.

But Dr. Packer is right. Galatians 3:28 may not answer the specific question of whether women may serve in the offices of the church, but its theology of their equality in Christ and the evidence of the changed attitude toward women does indeed require clear biblical justification to withhold from women the opportunity to exercise their gifts as elders and ministers. Unless this can be done, Galatians 3:28 is the Achilles' heel for those who oppose women in office.

3

The Parallel of Slavery

Galatians 3:28 plainly teaches there may be no discrimination between Jews and Greeks in the church. In Galatians 2:11–21 Paul makes it very clear that the old and powerful contrasts between circumcised and uncircumcised practiced in Jewish society have no place in the life of the Christian community. Circumcision is not necessary for membership in the church, nor may it be the basis for any inequality in the fellowship of the church. Nor were the uncircumcised restricted from serving in the offices of the church. The apostle Peter had led the church into accepting Gentiles after his encounter with Cornelius (Acts 10) and his consequent defense of the inclusion of the Gentiles in the church (Acts 11:1–18). After listening to Peter the apostles and brethren praised God saying, "So then, God has granted even the Gentiles repentance unto life."

Galatians 3:28 also affirms that in Christ there is no longer slave nor freeman in the church. That slaves could belong to Christ and therefore be members of the church had never been an issue. Peter in his sermon on Pentecost quoted Joel to have prophesied "even on my slaves, men and women, I will pour out my Spirit in those days" (Acts 2:18 JB).

Despite their equality in the church, Paul instructs slaves to obey and serve their masters. Their union in Christ did not end slave/master relationships in the Christian community as it abolished Jew/Gentile relations. He does teach that being in Christ significantly modifies their relations. These changes permeate his instructions to both.

It is out of this expediency for the sake of the gospel that Paul orders slaves to accept their status and to be obedient to their masters.

In 1 Timothy 6:2 Paul says that slaves are not to show less respect for their masters because they are brothers, but "instead, they are to serve them even better, because those who benefit from their service are believers, and dear to them." In his letter to Philemon, while acknowledging both Philemon and Onesimus as brothers in Christ, Paul sends Onesimus back to his slavery. In Titus 2:9–10 Paul instructs believing slaves to be witnesses to their (unbelieving?) masters by making the teaching about God our Savior attractive in every way.

Masters are likewise to treat their slaves in a brotherly fashion, without threatening them, knowing that "he who is both their Master and yours is in heaven, and there is no favoritism with him" (Eph. 6:9). In Colossians 4:1 masters are told to provide their slaves with what is right and fair. And Philemon, the master, is told to receive Onesimus, the slave, back as a dear brother in the Lord.

Paul's instructions to Christian slaves are clear, direct, and unconditional. The directives regarding slavery are as straightforward as they are for women to submit to their husbands (Eph. 5:22) and not to teach or have authority over men (1 Tim. 2:12). It was on the basis of these unambiguous imperatives that many Christians and even Reformed theologians as recently as the nineteenth century opposed the abolition of slavery.

Why does Paul so address slaves repeatedly in his letters to the churches? The answer lies readily at hand. Slaves who had become Christians understood that at the heart of the gospel was the reconciliation that God in Christ came to establish in the world through his kingdom manifest in the Christian church. They grasped that as Christians they possessed equality and liberty as brothers and sisters in their oneness "in Christ," even as Paul stated in Galatians 3:28. They understood that in the church the discriminating distinction between slave and master had been superseded by their unity in Christ.

So, then, why does Paul repeatedly instruct slaves to submit to their masters? What restrains Paul from demanding their equality as he does in the Jew/Greek relationship?

The answer is found in 1 Timothy 6:1 where Paul urges slaves to show their masters full respect on the ground "that God's name and our teaching may not be slandered." Paul's overriding concern was the gospel he preached. He feared it would be discredited as a revolutionary social and political message. He knew the violent response that revolt of slaves ignited in the Roman Empire. To oppose slavery would slander the gospel in the eyes of the world, hinder the proclamation of the Christian faith and the progress of the missionary program of the church, and incite great civil and political opposition against the church. It is out of this expediency for the sake of the gospel that Paul orders slaves to accept their status and to be obedient to their masters.

It was also true that Christian masters in all probability saw no sin in the institution of slavery that was integral to their society and, if they did, they feared the detrimental results of its sudden abolition. It would have been extremely difficult and unwise for Paul to have taught the immediate abolition of slavery even within the church. That Paul himself had a negative attitude toward slavery is evident from his condemnation of slave-traders. In 1 Timothy 1:10 he catalogues them with murderers, adulterers, perverts, liars, and perjurers. His attitude is evident in the advice he gives to slaves to take their freedom if they can (1 Cor. 7:21) and is felt in the tone of his letter to Philemon.

By stressing their common commitment to Christ and to each other the relations of masters and slaves are so revolutionized that in time slavery must become increasingly intolerable.

The inherently revolutionary character of the gospel would in time undermine the institution of slavery and lead to its abolition, not only in the church but also in society. To what extent Paul himself understood the full implications of his own teaching we do not know. But the roots for such a development lie within the passages that enjoin obedience on the part of slaves. As we have noted, by stressing their common commitment to Christ and to each other the relations of masters and slaves are so revolutionized that in time slavery must become increasingly intolerable. The letter to Philemon is especially instructive. Paul enjoins Philemon to receive Onesimus, a runaway slave, when he returns as a dear brother in the Lord. This is particularly telling because, in order to keep the system of slavery viable, the normal practice was for masters to severely punish returned slaves as a deterrent for others not to attempt to escape. Thus the epistle to Philemon is in fact a very revolutionary document that seriously undermines the foundation of slavery. Paul's instructions on slavery must be read as temporary, practical, and expedient injunctions that have no permanent validity.

It would take many centuries before slavery would be abolished in so-called Christian countries. Why did it take so long for the truth of our liberty in Christ to abolish the evil institution of slavery? An important factor was that the injunctions of Paul were read for centuries as permanent regulations that supported slavery. These directives were used by slave owners in the church to support slavery, which in turn contributed to perpetuating their interpretation for centuries. Eighteen centuries later these Pauline injunctions still remained the argument in defense of slavery in Confederate churches during the Civil War. Only as the church, under the prompting of the Holy Spirit, became more sensitive to the unity and equality in Christ of believers and the truth that God is no respecter of persons did the church, often reluctantly, promote and support the abolition of slavery.

Both proponents and opponents of women in office grant that the biblical imperatives on slavery must be read as culturally conditioned and relative directives that are not binding on the church today. All would agree that there remain implicit in these instructions principles that are universally valid and applicable to current employer-employee relationships. These principles continue to speak God's word to us in our social and economic circumstances.

Is there a parallel between the slave/master and male/female components of Galatians 3:28 that will help us resolve the problem of women in office?

There are several comparable elements that suggest such a parallel. As we have seen, in Galatians 3:28 the distinctions between slave and free and male and female, although they continue to exist, are superseded by equality in Christ in the church. The instructions in Paul's letters prominently modify the relations between slaves and masters, and between husbands and wives, as in Ephesians 5:22–33. Similarly Paul places restrictions on both slaves and women by instructing slaves to obey their masters and women to be subservient to their husbands and to refrain from exercising equality in the authoritative offices of the congregation.

What is of great significance is the parallelism between the grounds on which the apostle supports his instructions to both slaves and women. In 1 Timothy 6:1 he urges slaves to respect their masters "so that God's name and our teaching may not be slandered." In Titus 2:5 he requires women to be subject to their husbands "so that no one will malign the word of God." Various translations make the comparison with 1 Timothy 6:1 very clear. The Revised Standard Version reads "that the word of God may not be discredited"; the New English Bible, "Thus the Gospel will not be brought into disrepute"; the Jerusalem Bible, "so that the message of God is never disgraced"; and the American Standard Version, "that the word of God be not blasphemed."

What is of great significance is the parallelism between the grounds on which the apostle supports his instructions to both slaves and women.

Proponents of women in office see the parallel instructive on how to interpret the Scriptures to resolve the dilemma of the two lines of thought about women in the New Testament. Opponents acknowledge that the gospel made significant changes both in the slave/master and the male/female relationships. They would affirm that the status of women in marriage and in the church has been infused with the ameliorating influence of the gospel's teaching on the unity of all believers in Christ.

But although they accept the temporary and relativizing character of the commands for slaves to obey their masters, they interpret the instructions for women to be subservient in both home and church as permanent, universal imperatives applicable to all times and places. Is this distinction valid? On what basis can opponents defend the breakdown of the parallel? How can opponents of women in office justify relativizing the clear injunctions of Paul regarding slavery but not the instructions regarding women?

How can opponents of women in office justify relativizing the clear injunctions of Paul regarding slavery but not the instructions regarding women?

George W. Knight III cites three considerations why the directives concerning slavery are not to be interpreted as permanently binding (*The New Testament Teaching on the Role Relationship of Men and Women,* pp. 22–24). First, slavery as an institution is nowhere taught in the Scriptures as ordained by God. Second, according to 1 Corinthians 7:20, "Each one should remain in the situation which he was in when God called him." Paul is directing slaves on how to conduct themselves in the situation in which they find themselves, but he is not thereby establishing or endorsing slavery, for in verse 21 he advises that they should accept their freedom if possible. Third, Paul is prepared to compromise the ideal in view of the human imperfections remaining in Christians, as Moses permitted divorce, according to Jesus, because of the Jews' hardness of heart.

It is readily apparent that Knight's second and third considerations could be applied with equal warrant to relativize the prohibition against women teaching and having authority in the church. Paul could be instructing women to accept male domination in the church as they experienced subordination in the family and society, without thereby teaching that their subservience was a permanent aspect of their role in the church. He might likewise be willing to tolerate their inequality in the church as he does for slaves, for the purpose of avoiding the offense that would hinder the furtherance of the gospel in society. We might conclude that the apostle was willing in deference to the weakness of males who would think their dominance in their homes and society threatened by the equality of women in the life of the church to forbid women from equality in the offices of the congregation. These two considerations could be used to defend the temporary nature of Paul's restrictions on women.

It is Knight's first consideration that brings us to the crux of the issue regarding women in office. The subservience of women is a creation ordinance on which the apostle Paul grounds his restraints on women in the church. In 1 Timothy 2:12 and in 1 Corinthians 11:8 he cites the second creation account (Gen. 2:21–23) in defense of his prohibitions. In the judgment of Knight and the opponents the parallel between slavery and the subordination of women breaks down at this point.

Opponents have called 1 Timothy 2:12 the "Rock of Gibraltar" on which the case for women in office is lost.

Opponents have called 1 Timothy 2:12 the "Rock of Gibraltar" on which the case for women in office is lost. As one opponent writes: "No one verse in Scripture speaks more clearly or more decisively to the question whether women ought to be ordained to serve as ministers than I Timothy 2:12" (Norman Shepherd, *Women in the Service of Christ*, p. 6). We must therefore turn to a careful consideration of 1 Timothy 2:11–15, along with 1 Corinthians 11:3–16 and 14:33–36.

4

The Prohibition of
1 Timothy 2:11–15

The only New Testament passage that speaks directly to the issue of women functioning as teachers and authorities in the church is 1 Timothy 2:11–15. Verses 11–12 read: "A woman should learn in quietness and full submission. I do not permit a woman to teach or to have authority over a man; she must be silent." These words appear to forbid the ordination of women as ministers (who officially teach) and women as elders (who exercise authority). If so, the equality in Christ taught in Galatians 3:28 does not include equality of function for women in the church. How valid this reading is, we will consider later.

The singular importance of 1 Timothy 2:11–15 lies in its appeal to the authority of the Old Testament to undergird the ordinance not to permit a woman to teach and have authority over a man. In verses 13–14 Paul writes, "For

Adam was formed first, then Eve. And Adam was not the one deceived; it was the woman who was deceived and became a sinner." It is the universal truths of creation and the fall that seem to give normative and timeless status to the Pauline prohibitions. Paul's arguments from Genesis appear to root his ordinances in God-ordained, inviolable realities of human existence. As noted at the end of the previous chapter, according to opposing critics, it is the creation ordinance of women's subordination to men that confirms the argument against women serving in the official offices of the church.

> *Practical instructions in the Bible that concern behavior and conduct must be understood and evaluated, and their permanent validity ascertained in the light of the doctrinal teaching of the Scriptures.*

Before we proceed it is important to remember an obvious and fundamental principle of interpretation. Practical instructions in the Bible that concern behavior and conduct must be understood and evaluated, and their permanent validity ascertained in the light of the doctrinal teaching of the Scriptures. Doctrinal truths shape, define, and validate the norms to which the church seeks to be obedient and not the other way around. The imperatives on slavery are no longer applicable in the light of the truth that

Christ has abolished such demeaning distinctions, although in that same light we may learn permanent lessons from these imperatives for employer-employee relations. Paul's instructions on hair styles are not binding in our times because they are not rooted in a doctrinal foundation, although from these instructions we may learn how sexual distinctions are not to be confused. The command to love one another and even our enemies is valid for all time because it is a corollary of the gospel truth of God's love for all people.

So unless it is clear that Paul is restricting the teaching of Galatians 3:28 in 1 Timothy 2:11–15 on the ground of other biblical truths, the biblical teaching of the unity and equality of men and women is the norm by which the church should be guided in its life and practice regarding women serving in the church's administrative offices, and the practical prohibitions read in that light. To the arguments from creation and the fall we must give our attention.

The first ground Paul advances to prohibit women from teaching and wielding authority in the church is the priority of Adam's creation, "for Adam was formed first, then Eve." The reference is not to Genesis 1:27–28, which reads, "So God created man in his own image, in the image of God he created him; male and female he created them. God blessed them and said to them, 'Be fruitful and increase in number; fill the earth and subdue it. Rule over the fish of the sea and the birds of the air and over every living creature that moves on the ground.'" In this passage no distinction is made between male and female in their creation (both are in the image of God), nor in their authority (both are mandated to rule over all things).

The reference is to Genesis 2, where Adam was created first and God placed him in the Garden of Eden to work it and to take care of it. Adam received the command not to eat of the tree of the knowledge of good and evil. Then we read in verse 18, "The LORD God said, 'It is not good for the man to be alone. I will make a helper suitable for him." In verses 20–23, we are told, "So the LORD God caused the man to fall into a deep sleep; and while he was sleeping, he took one of the man's ribs and closed up the place with flesh. Then the LORD God made a woman from the rib he had taken out of the man, and he brought her to the man. The man said, 'This is now bone of my bones and flesh of my flesh; she shall be called 'woman' for she was taken out of man.' For this reason a man will leave his father and mother and be united to his wife, and they will become one flesh."

The account teaches that man was created before woman and woman was made from man. Some consequently reason that woman is therefore subordinate to man. But the fact that Adam was created before Eve in itself does not argue for man's priority over woman. As John Calvin observes, "Paul's argument that woman is subject because she was created second, does not seem to be very strong, for John the Baptist went before Christ in time and yet was far inferior to Him" (Calvin's New Testament Commentaries, *Commentary on I Timothy,* p. 217). The argument rests on the supposition that Eve was made to be an appendage to serve Adam as a "suitable helper," thereby establishing woman's subservience to man.

In one form or another the inferiority and unsuitability of women to occupy positions of leadership and authority have been frequently maintained on the basis of the second creation account, as Paul apparently does in 1 Timothy 2:13. Dr. William Hendricksen writes:

But in his sovereign wisdom God made the human pair in such a manner that it is natural for *him* to lead, for *her* to follow; for *him* to be aggressive, for *her* to be receptive; for *him* to invent, for *her* to use the tools which he invents. The tendency *to follow* was embedded in Eve's very soul as she came forth from the hand of her Creator. Hence, it would not be right to reverse this order in public worship. Why should a woman be encouraged to do things that are contrary to her nature? . . . It is when the woman recognizes this basic distinction and acts accordingly that she can be a blessing to the man, can exert a gracious yet very powerful and beneficent influence upon him and can promote her own happiness unto God's glory. (New Testament Commentary, *Exposition of the Pastoral Epistles,* pp. 109–10)

But does the Genesis account teach woman's subordination to man as an appendage created for him? The words "suitable helper" are a translation of two Hebrew words. The word for "helper" translates the word *ezer,* which is used in the Old Testament most often of God helping man as in Exodus 18:4; Deuteronomy 33:29; Psalms 33:20; 70:5; 115:9, 19, 11, and is never used elsewhere to designate a subordinate. The Hebrew word *neged,* which is translated "suitable," means literally "according to what is in front of" or "corresponding to." In the Brown, Driver, and Briggs lexicon, verse 18 is quoted as reading: "I will make him a help corresponding to him i.e. equal and adequate to himself" (p. 617).

That the woman is called "helper" in Genesis 2:18 does not mean that she is thereby inferior or subject to the man whom she was made to help.

That the woman is called "helper" in Genesis 2:18 does not mean that she is thereby inferior or subject to the man whom she was made to help. Rather, Eve as the helper is to be thought of as a co-worker or enabler, who serves as an equal partner with Adam. The fact that Eve was made from Adam's rib suggests a side-by-side relationship of parity, not one of hierarchy or subordination, a parity that is further supported by the equality expressed in "bone of my bone, and flesh of my flesh." Verse 24 stresses that woman is so essentially the counterpart of man that he will sacrifice his relationship to his parents to be united with his wife. This unity is one of equals ("they will become one flesh"), a created partnership rather than she serving as an appendage. The verse is the more significant because in the ancient patriarchal society and in many parts of the world to this day, where women are considered subordinate, the woman leaves her parents to join her husband in his home. How else can this strange reversal from the practice of ancient society be accounted for in this text than as a revelation of marriage as an equal partnership?

How else can this strange reversal from the practice of ancient society be accounted for in this text than as a revelation of marriage as an equal partnership?

The apostle's argument from Genesis 2 is without support in the text. The two accounts of God's creation of woman convey the complete partnership of man and woman and in no way teaches woman's inferiority or subordination to man. This is not to say that Paul was in error when he adduces his argument from Genesis, as we shall see.

Paul uses the same argument for man's priority over woman in 1 Corinthians 11:8 where he writes, "For man did not come from woman, but woman from man, neither was man created for woman, but woman for man." But he immediately counterbalances the argument in verses 11–12: "In the Lord, however, woman is not independent of man, nor is man independent of woman. For as woman came from man, so also man is born of woman." The juxtaposition of these two statements suggests the apostle's awareness of the limitation of the argument from Genesis. He has reference to more than the biological fact that sons are born of mothers. The phrase "in the Lord" means to be in the realm of the lordship of the exalted Christ, manifest in the church of Christ. In that kingdom of Christ's lordship male and female have an interdependence in their oneness in Christ, the same basis on which the apostle grounds their equality in Galatians 3:28.

First Corinthians 11:8–12 is an example of Paul "fighting on two fronts," as Professor F. W. Grosheide called it. On the one hand Paul writes in verse 8 in the vein of accepted male priority and authority over woman in harmony with the biblical understanding of his day and as he no doubt had been taught as a rabbi prior to his conversion. But on the other hand he acknowledges in verses 11–12 the changed relations between male and female "in Christ" as he taught in Galatians 3:28.

Paul's use of the second creation account rests on an interpretation of the passage supplemented by Genesis 3:16, where Eve is told that her husband "will rule over you." Her subjection to her husband is stated as part of the curse upon the woman for her fall into sin. Opponents argue that man's rule over woman is implicit in Genesis 2 and that in Genesis 3 as a punishment for her sin she will be under the domineering and oppressive rule of her sinful husband. But, as we have noted, there is nothing in Genesis 2 that teaches woman's subordination to man, and to read it into the text from Genesis 3:16 is without textual and contextual warrant.

It is a harmonizing conjecture on the part of opponents to support their preconceived position. Opponents argue that just as Genesis 3 presumes the reality of childbearing from Genesis 1:28 and 2:24, and the reality of work from Genesis 2:15 when it pronounces the effects of the fall and sin as resulting in the pain of childbearing (Gen. 3:16) and painful toil (Gen. 3:17–19), so the rule of the husband is presumed in Genesis 3:16 from Genesis 2:18–25 (see George W. Knight III, *The New Testament Teaching on the Role Relationship of Men and Women*, pp. 43–44). But for the parallel to be warranted, Genesis 3:16 should read in some such fashion as "and he will rule over you as a master" or "he will rule domineeringly over you." The text simply states, "he will rule over you," which is the curse pronounced upon the woman for what she has done.

Whatever validity Paul's argument in 1 Timothy 2:13 on Adam's priority had for his readers, it does not appear to be a valid ground on which we may justify prohibiting women from functioning in the offices of the church today.

The second ground Paul cites in 1 Timothy 2:14 in defense of his instruction is based on the role of Eve in the fall. "And Adam was not the one deceived; it was the woman who was deceived and became a sinner." The point of the argument appears to be that Eve succumbed to the serpent's temptation because she was more easily deceived and therefore women are by nature less competent to be entrusted with teaching and authority.

It is understandable that opponents hesitate in today's society to affirm the inferiority of women to serve as leaders. One opponent hastens to say, *without citing any scriptural warrant for his statement* (Norman Shepherd, *Women in the Service of Christ*, p. 9): "It is essential to note at the outset that the rationale Paul offers has nothing to do with some sort of presumed female inferiority. It is not that women lack the spiritual, intellectual, or emotional capacity to function as leaders and teachers. It is not that they lack the skills required of officeholders. The rationale can in no sense be construed as a putdown for women."

Opponents are somewhat at a loss to explain the significance of this argument. One writes: "Paul does not expand and develop this argument, and we must be content with his brief statement of it. One may conjecture that the apostle cites this foundational incident to indicate that when the roles established by God in creation were reversed by Eve, it manifestly had a disastrous effect" (George W. Knight III, *The New Testament Teaching on the Role Relationship of Men and Women*, p. 31). In similar fashion, Dr. Hendricksen interprets the text to teach that Eve's fall occurred when she ignored her divinely ordained position to follow and chose to lead and so sinned. Thus, she must now obey her sinful husband, no longer an unmixed blessing as it was before the fall. The conjecture assumes, of course, the subordinate role established by Adam's priority in creation, which we have called into question.

John Calvin says that Paul is referring to the punishment inflicted upon the woman (Gen. 3:16) by which she is "deprived of all her freedom and placed under the yoke." He writes: "the apostle does not base his argument simply or merely on the cause of the transgression, but on the sentence pronounced upon it by God" (Calvin's New Testament Commentaries, *Commentary on I Timothy*, p. 218).

But for Paul to base his argument on this proposed explanation of Eve's punishment raises a disturbing theological problem. Why is the punishment for Eve's sin not lifted from women by the atoning work of Christ? It is a fundamental teaching of Romans that "just as the result of one trespass was condemnation for all men, so also the result of one act of righteousness was justification that brings life for all men" (5:18). Through Christ's atoning death and victorious resurrection we are freed from the curse of the fall. Although the effects of the curse may continue, it is imperative that in harmony with Christ's redeeming work we do all that is possible to remove the effects of sin. Does not the same apply to the subordination of women, which on the basis of Genesis 3:16 is one of the results of the fall? Is it not imperative that in harmony with Christ's redeeming work, we do all that is possible to remove the effects of the curse on Eve from marriages, in societies, and especially within the church?

> *Is it not imperative that in harmony with Christ's redeeming work, we do all that is possible to remove the effects of the curse on Eve from marriages, in societies, and especially within the church?*

In this connection between the curse on Eve for her sin and the subordination of women through Eve's sin in 1 Timothy 2:14, we may reflect on the significance of the amazing fact that after his resurrection Jesus chose to reveal himself first to the women who came to the tomb and then commissioned them to bring the good news of his resurrection to his male disciples (Matt. 28:7, 10; Mark 16:7; Luke 24:9; John 20:2). This commissioning was the more remarkable because in that day women were not considered qualified to bear legal witness.

What is the profound divine truth revealed by the fact that Jesus chose women to be the initial witnesses to his resurrection, the foundational truth on which all Christian proclamation rests, and instructed them to bring the good news of the resurrection to the disciples? In 1 Timothy 2:14 Paul adduces what was the current view of the Genesis account of the fall in which Eve is the primary spoiler of the creation by being deceived and thereby introduced sin into the world ("she became a sinner"). Thereupon she brought upon herself and all her daughters, as punishment for her sin, the subordination of women to men. In the presence of that reality the resurrection of Jesus marks the beginning of the new creation. Women appear at the beginning of the new age, as Eve appeared at the beginning of the first creation. Eve's transgression placed her under the curse of humiliating subservience. With the resurrection of the Second Adam the new creation has come; the curse on the old creation is lifted by the atoning death and resurrection of Jesus. "He was delivered over to death for our sins and was raised to life for our justification" (Rom. 4:25).

The risen Christ signals the new creation by elevating woman to her renewed status of equality by authorizing her to be the first to proclaim his resurrection. If Eve was the first to spoil the original creation, Eve's daughters at the tomb are the first to herald the coming of the renewed creation. If Eve was cursed for her sin to be subordinate to

Adam, by the Christ event Eve's daughters are reinstated to their pristine role of partnership and equality. What better account can we give for the astonishing role of the women at the empty tomb and their divine commission to testify to the male disciples of the resurrection of the Christ? In the New Testament church the curse is abolished and in Christ there is no longer the hierarchy of male over female. The practice of Jesus to relate equally to men and women was vindicated by his divine resurrection.

> *The risen Christ signals the new creation by elevating woman to her renewed status of equality by authorizing her to be the first to proclaim his resurrection.*

If Paul's first argument of Adam's priority does not justify prohibiting women from teaching and exercising authority in the church, and the second argument is likewise wanting in scriptural authority, what may we conclude about Paul's use of Scripture to undergird his restriction on women teaching and ruling in the church?

To propose that Paul was wrong in his application of Scripture and therefore wrong to deny women the opportunity to serve as teachers and authorities is to call into question the inspiration and authority of the apostle. Such a conclusion is not an option for the believer committed to the Reformed confession of the Scriptures as the Word of God. How can the difficulty be resolved in keeping with our confession of the Bible to be divinely inspired and our commitment to the Scriptures as infallible in faith and practice?

The appearance of 1 Timothy 2:11–15 as well as 1 Corinthians 11:3–16 and 14:33–35 in the New Testament comes as something of a surprise. One has come to expect, from the example of Jesus in the Gospels, the inclusiveness of Pentecost, and the role of women in the early church as reported in the Acts of the Apostles and in the letters of Paul, the full equality of women and men. These restrictive passages in Timothy and Corinthians appear inconsistent with the basic New Testament teaching on the equality of men and women in Christ epitomized in Galatians 3:28.

These prohibitive regulations appear in marked contrast to what the apostle writes in Colossians 3:16 ("Let the word of Christ dwell in you richly as you teach and admonish one another with all wisdom, and as you sing psalms, hymns and spiritual songs with gratitude in your hearts to God") and in Ephesians 5:19 ("Speak to one another with psalms, hymns and spiritual songs"). Both passages have to do with worshiping assemblies as does 1 Timothy 2:11–15. The directives of 1 Peter 4:10–11 seem very much in tension with the restrictive passages when we read, with no qualifications of gender, "Each one should use whatever gift he has received to serve others, faithfully administering God's grace in its various forms. If anyone speaks, he should do it as one speaking the very words of God. If anyone serves he should do it with the strength God provides, so that in all things God may be praised through Jesus Christ." And not least, the prohibitions seem incongruous when reading 1 Corinthians 12, where the diversity of spiritual gifts and their employment for the unity of the church are so magnificently portrayed with no restrictions of gender.

As is required of all responsible interpretation, 1 Timothy 2:11–15 must be read in context. It is readily apparent that the letters of 1 and 2 Timothy were sent to instruct and encourage Timothy, the young associate of Paul, in his vexing and difficult task of ministering in the troubled church of Ephesus. The apostle Paul in 1 Timothy 1:3 reminds Timothy that he had urged him to stay in Ephesus "so that you may command certain men not to teach false doctrines any longer nor to devote themselves to myths and endless genealogies." In his farewell address to the elders of the church in Ephesus Paul had prophesied: "I know that after I leave, savage wolves will come in among you and will not spare the flock. Even from your own number men will arise and distort the truth in order to draw away disciples after them. So be on your guard" (Acts 20:29–31). Paul's concern was well founded, for it is evident that Timothy was assigned to combat aggressive, false teachers in the congregation, some of them straying elders, who were seriously disrupting the church and threatening its existence.

The apostle characterizes these false teachers as those who have wandered from a pure heart, good conscience, and sincere faith to meaningless talk, wanting to be teachers of the law but not knowing what they are talking about (1:6–7); who have shipwrecked their faith (1:19–20); who abandon the faith and follow deceiving spirits and things taught by demons (4:1–3); who peddle godless myths and old wives' tales (4:7). In 6:3–5 Paul reprimands the false teachers who are conceited and understand nothing, who have an unhealthy interest in controversies and arguments that result in envy, quarreling, malicious talk, evil suspicions, and constant friction, and who think that godliness is a means to financial gain. Apparently these heretical teachers were corrupting the gospel by seeking to mix and blend it with pagan philosophies and false religions that were current in Ephesian society, and thereby in fact destroying the gospel.

Second Timothy 3:6–7 states that these false teachers "worm their way into homes and gain control over weak-willed women, who are loaded down with sins and are swayed by all kinds of evil desires, always learning but never able to acknowledge the truth." These heretical leaders evoked and inflamed these credulous women to aggressive and troublesome conduct in the Ephesian church, which accounts for the extended treatment about the proper demeanor of women in worship in 1 Timothy 2:9–15, and the considerable advice about women in 5:2–16.

It is in response to these wayward men and women that Paul issues directives to restore proper behavior in worship in chapter 2, and to establish competent leadership in the church in chapter 3. As he says in 1 Timothy 3:14–15, "I am writing you these instructions so that, if I am delayed, you will know how people ought to conduct themselves in God's household."

First Timothy 2 addresses matters that have to do with the church in its worship. In verses 1–7 Paul urges the church to intercede for all people in its prayers, which suggests there was some exclusiveness with which the church was struggling that the apostle is concerned to correct. His awareness of errant teachers, who were challenging his teaching, appears in the defensiveness that is evident in verse 7 when he stresses his authority as an apostle to teach the true faith. Verse 8 calls for men "to lift up holy hands in prayer" with pure and sincere hearts, without engaging in the quarrels and disputes aroused by false teaching. In verses 9–10 Paul urges women to dress modestly in a manner befitting godly women at worship, not as women who live for pleasure. It should be noted that in each instance the occasion for the instruction is conditions that require correction. We would anticipate the same is true for verses 11–14.

In verse 11 Paul states that a woman should learn in quietness and full submission. In Judaism women could not be directly involved in worship. They might attend the services as observers to listen but not to learn and teach. Paul encourages women as participants to learn, even as Jesus commended Mary for her interest in his teaching (Luke 10:42). In verses 11 and 12 the word "woman," which in the original Greek may refer to either a single woman or to a wife, probably refers to women in general for verses 8–10 speak of men and women. If so, women in "full submission" are instructed to show deference to men by remaining silent in the church.

What Paul is prohibiting by his injunction for women to learn in quietness or in silence is a matter of some debate. The text has been interpreted to restrict women to total silence, even to deny them the right to sing in the worship services. Others interpret it to mean that women may not do any speaking in the congregation during the worship services, for the demand for silence prohibits any teaching (2:12) or praying (2:8) or even questions (1 Cor. 14:35).

It is doubtful that the silence enjoined in the text is intended to be rigorously interpreted. The word used in the Greek connotes quietness and peacefulness rather then total silence. It is highly unlikely that Paul intended this injunction to be literally observed in all circumstances. In Ephesians 5:19–20, both men and women are to "Speak to one another with psalms, hymns and spiritual songs. Sing and make music in your heart to the Lord, always giving thanks to God the Father for everything in the name of our Lord Jesus Christ." The same holds for Colossians 3:16, where believers are told to "teach and admonish one another with all wisdom." Of particular importance is 1 Corinthians 11:5, where Paul speaks of women who pray and prophesy in the worship service, requiring only that their heads be covered. If he had thought it wrong for these women to speak he would simply have forbidden their participation instead of discussing what they should be doing with their heads.

It is doubtful that the silence enjoined in the text is intended to be rigorously interpreted.

In the church of Ephesus there were younger widows who had become idlers, going about from house to house as gossips and busybodies, saying inappropriate things, and in fact turning away to follow Satan (1 Tim. 5:12–15). The instructions on prayer and dress (vv. 1–10) were given in response to improper behavior. It is reasonable, then, to expect that Paul found it necessary to restrain women in the congregation. Women who were influenced by the false teachers and feeling themselves emancipated by their freedom in the gospel, engaged in noisy, disruptive, and offensive behavior in the worship services, parading their new status in a usurping, domineering attitude toward the men in the congregation. This would account for Paul continuing in verse 12: "I do not permit a woman to teach or to have authority over a man; she must be silent."

Several matters complicate the interpretation of verse 12. What is meant by "teaching" and "authority?" How are teaching and authority related?

There is no unanimity among opponents of women in office on precisely what the apostle is banning in verse 12. Some interpret the prohibition to mean that a woman may not do any teaching in the church when males are present because she must be in full submission. This is the official position of the Orthodox Presbyterian Church. In 1990 the General Assembly decided on the basis of 1 Timothy 2:12 that it was wrong for a woman to teach Bible studies even in a home when a male is present if she does so under the auspices of the church. This would appear to be the most natural, literal reading of the injunction.

In the Christian Reformed Church opponents have generally maintained that a distinction must be made between preaching or teaching in an official manner by an ordained minister in a worship service and other types of teaching. Few have any qualms about women teaching church school classes, adult Bible classes, high school and college Bible courses, or even seminary students. One writer summarizes the passage to say: "What Paul does not permit is the authoritative teaching that takes place in the worship when the minister preaches a sermon. It is official authority, the authority of the eldership, and of those elders who are charged with the work of preaching and teaching" (Norman Shepherd, *Women in the Service of the Christ,* p. 8).

It is appropriate to assume that if women are encouraged to learn they should be permitted to teach.

What type of teaching is Paul forbidding women? It is appropriate to assume that if women are encouraged to learn they should be permitted to teach. And in fact it is clear that women engaged in teaching, with the encouragement of the apostle. Priscilla with her husband, Aquila, instructed Apollos into a fuller understanding of the faith

(Acts 18:26). Women such as Phoebe (Rom. 16:1–3), Euodia, and Syntyche (Phil. 4:2–3), as co-workers with Paul, were in all likelihood engaged in teaching, along with men such as Clement. In Titus 2:3 older women are told "to teach what is good" to younger women. We must mention once again Colossians 3:16, where Paul includes among elements of worship, "Let the word of Christ dwell in you richly as you teach and admonish one another with all wisdom," and 1 Corinthians 11:5 where women pray and prophesy, a form of teaching, in the assembly at worship.

There is evidence in the New Testament that by the time the Pastoral Letters were written, the teaching function in the church was becoming more "official" and associated with certain persons, such as Timothy, Epaphras, and appointed teachers (1 Cor. 12:28). In 1 Timothy 5:17 we read that "elders who direct the affairs of the church well are worthy of double honor, especially those whose work is preaching and teaching." It may well be that Paul is restricting women from this type of official teaching in the Ephesian church and in all the congregations (1 Cor. 14:33). In the light of the turmoil in the Ephesian church and in all churches it is likely that Paul had this kind of teaching in mind.

What is meant by the phrase "or to have authority over a man"? The Greek word *authentein,* translated "authority," appears only this one time in the New Testament, and thus its meaning in this context is unsure. It is generally agreed that *authentein* means more than simply having authority; it means "to have dominion" as it is translated in the American Standard Version, or "to domineer" as in the New English Bible, or "to dictate" as in Moffatt's translation. Dibelius translates it "interrupt." The King James Version renders it "usurp authority," suggesting the exercise of illegitimate authority by force.

Scholars report that recently it has been confirmed from the use of the word in Greek literature that it has to do with a domineering, authoritarian power rather than with what is normally associated with authority, although they report that by New Testament times the word was being used with the more general meaning of "authority." If the apostle had used *exousia,* the word he employs for "authority" in 1 Corinthians 11:10, or *kurieuō,* the word he uses for "to lord over" in 2 Corinthians 1:24, it would have meant he simply had in mind that women are not to exercise an authority that contradicts their subordination. But it cannot be ignored that Paul chose the word *authentein.* The choice of this obscure word suggests that Paul uses *authentein* deliberately because he is concerned about those women who sought to exercise a dominating, domineering authority over men.

An additional uncertainty in the text is the relationship between the two clauses joined by "or": "to teach *or* have authority over a man." Is Paul distinguishing two separate functions: the teaching function we associate with ministers and the leadership function of elders? Or is he speaking about authoritative teaching? The two functions are closely related. Elders are expected to be "able to teach" (3:2).

Paul is forbidding a woman from domineering teaching that would be highly offensive in a male-dominated society.

It would appear to be an acceptable interpretation that Paul is forbidding a woman from domineering teaching that would be highly offensive in a male-dominated society. What gives credence to this interpretation is the context of the aggressive, troublesome women "ever learning but never able to acknowledge the truth" who nonetheless pretended to teach or interrupted the teaching and so troubled the church in its worship. In that situation Paul issues his blanket restriction. If so, verse 12 may not be denying women everywhere and always the right to teach authoritatively in the offices of minister and elder, but rather clarifying that they should not be allowed to do so without competence nor in a way that seeks to lord it over males.

The issue of authority in teaching is less relevant today than it was in Paul's lifetime. Prior to the formation of the New Testament canon, teaching was dependent on the qualification, reliability, and authorization of the teacher. Today all teaching of the Word of God is based on the Bible and therefore is authoritative, irrespective of who the teacher is, because the authority lies in the Word, and thus in God himself, and not in the teacher, whether woman or man. At this point it is clear from verse 12 that the women in Ephesus were not allowed to engage in a form of teaching that gave them dominance over the men in the church.

All teaching of the Word of God is based on the Bible and therefore is authoritative, irrespective of who the teacher is.

Before we try to discern whether the restrictions are intended to be normative for the church of all ages, we need to give due attention to the primary purpose and intent of the apostle in writing his letter to Timothy. Paul's intent was to give practical instructions for the peace and good order of the church in the critical situation that existed in the early church. The problem as it applied to women arose on the one hand out of the new liberty and role women were given in the church in the light of the gospel. And on the other hand the problem arose out of the conflict of that teaching with the dominant cultural position, both among the Jews and Greeks, of male superiority and woman's subservience.

The presence of this conflict in the church was damaging to both the well-being of the congregation and the witness to the gospel in the world. Paul's epistles to Timothy are not general, all-purpose letters on church organization and polity as, for example, the epistle to the Romans, which addresses Christian doctrine and life. The instructions of 1 Timothy are directives to deal with the difficulties in Ephesus, as well as in other churches in the New Testament era, which arose out of the conflict between the teaching of the gospel and the prevailing cultural conventions, especially as the conflict collided with the furtherance of the gospel. These restraints are not then necessarily meant to be literally observed by the church of all ages and in all places.

Paul's overriding concern is the progress of the gospel. For the great missionary apostle, his first and foremost concern was the spread of the gospel throughout the whole world. This dominant concern permeates all his letters. He rejoices that the faith of the Romans "is being reported all over the world" (Rom. 1:8). To the Corinthians he writes: "I resolved to know nothing while I was with you except Jesus Christ and him crucified" (1 Cor. 2:2). His being in prison encouraged others to preach Christ, some of them out of ignoble ambitions and vicious motives, but the single-minded apostle cries out: "But what does it matter? The important thing is that in every way, whether from false motives or true, Christ is preached. And because of this I rejoice" (Phil. 1:18).

> ## *Paul's overriding concern is the progress of the gospel.*

We have already observed this paramount concern elicits his directives for slaves. In 1 Timothy 6:1 he appeals for the obedience of slaves for the sake of the gospel ("so that God's name and our teaching may not be slandered"). Paul knew the devastating barriers that would be erected against the gospel if it were to be identified with the abolition of slavery. That he was not unaware of the incompatibility of the gospel with slavery can be detected throughout his letters.

In the light of our entire discussion thus far, we may believe it was the same concern for the advancement of the gospel that occasioned the Pauline passages on women's subordination. In Titus 2:5, Paul supports the subjection of women to their husbands "so that no one will malign the word of God." Paul is in line with the whole of the New Testament. The same concern for the furtherance of the gospel is highlighted in 1 Peter 3:1–2, when women are instructed to be submissive to their husbands "so that, if any of them do not believe the word, they may be won over without talk by the behavior of their wives, when they see the purity and reverence of your lives." The apostle Paul knew the insurmountable obstacle and resistance that would be raised against the gospel were it to be identified as a feminist movement. As in the instance of slavery, for the gospel to be identified with feminine equality in the dominant male society of the times would have characterized the church as a political and societal revolutionary movement. From a human point of view, it would have incited society and the authorities to so violently oppose the gospel as to completely destroy it. Again, as in the case of slavery, we observe throughout the New Testament the same incompatibility of the gospel with the subservience of women and sense the lifting of the subjugation of women in the church and in the home. The teaching in Ephesians 5:21–33 of mutual submission, and husbands loving their wives as much as they love their own bodies is a far cry from the stern announcement of Genesis 3:16 that the husband will rule over his wife.

Paul knew the insurmountable obstacle and resistance that would be raised against the gospel were it to be identified as a feminist movement.

We may in all reverence assume Jesus chose from among his disciples, who included both men and women, twelve male disciples to be the apostles out of consideration for the offense and confrontation that would have resulted to the gospel in the male-dominated society of the first century. It may be noted that Jesus never raised his voice against slavery. Jesus was not insensitive to the impropriety of generating unnecessary hostility and opposition that would sacrifice the central thrust of the gospel. Therefore, to elevate our Lord's selection of an all-male apostolate to a prescription for all time is as unwarranted as it would be to insist that the Christian ministry must be Jewish in perpetuity because the first apostles were all Jews.

The perspective on 1 Timothy 2:12–15 that it need not be understood as a permanent and universal ordinance to be observed by the church in perpetuity, is substantiated by 1 Corinthians 14, which parallels the Timothy passage and deals with the problems occasioned by women in the worship services of the Corinthian church. For our purposes we need not go into a discussion of this passage, but do well to take note of what John Calvin says about it in his commentary on First Corinthians. He makes several comments on the relevant passages suggesting that while he generally reads the texts in the traditional way of women's subordination to men in the church, he does not interpret Paul's injunctions as hard and fast rules to be observed by the church today.

On 1 Corinthians 14:33–34, a passage analogous to 1 Timothy 2:11–15, "As in all congregations of the saints, women should remain silent in the churches. They are not allowed to speak, but must remain in submission, as the law says," Calvin allows expediency to determine the practice, rather than referring to the authority of Genesis. He comments (Calvin's New Testament Commentaries, *Commentary on I Corinthians,* p. 306; emphasis added):

> It appears that the Corinthian church was also spoiled by this fault, that when they met together, there was a place for the chattering women, or rather it was allowed great liberty. Paul accordingly forbids them to speak in public, either by way of teaching or prophesying. *But we should understand*

this as referring to the situation where things can be done in the regular way, or where the Church is well established. For a situation can arise where there is a need of such a kind as calls for a woman to speak. But Paul is confining himself to what is fitting in a properly organized congregation.

In commenting on 1 Corinthians 14:35, which reads, "If they [women] want to inquire about something, they should ask their own husbands at home; for it is disgraceful for a woman to speak in the church," Calvin writes (Calvin's New Testament Commentaries, *Commentary on I Corinthians,* p. 309; emphasis added):

But as he is discussing the external organization *(externa politia)* here, it is enough for his purpose to point out what is unseemly, so that the Corinthians might avoid it. *However, the discerning reader should come to the decision that the things which Paul is dealing with here are indifferent, neither good nor bad, and that they are forbidden only because they work against seemliness and edification.*

Here Calvin clearly states that the ground for prohibiting women from speaking in the church, in marked contrast to 1 Timothy 2:11–12, is because in the situation that existed at the time it would be contrary to accepted propriety and thus a hindrance to the welfare of the congregation.

Calvin's commentary on Paul's injunction in verse 40, "Let all things be done decently and in order," is most striking and relevant to the approach and position of this book (Calvin's New Testament Commentaries, *Commentary on I Corinthians,* p. 310; emphasis added):

This conclusion is more general, for not only does it sum up the whole situation in a few words, but also the different aspects of it. And more than that, it provides us with a suitable standard for assessing everything connected with external organization *(ad externam politiam)*. Since he had dealt with rites in various passages, he wanted, at this point to sum everything up very briefly, viz. that seemliness should be preserved, and disorder should be avoided. *This statement shows that he was not willing to put people's consciences under obligation to the instructions he gave above, as if they were binding for their own sake, but only in so far as they make for seemliness and peace.* For this we acquire (as I have said) a general principle, which tells us the purpose which the organization of the Church *(Ecclesiae politia)* ought to be serving.

In light of the above comments, it is evident that Calvin does not conceive of the Pauline injunctions as inviolable principles to be observed in all ages and under all circumstances. The selection of these quotations from Calvin is not intended to imply that he differs from the traditional interpretations associated with these passages in his commentaries, for he does not. But they do demonstrate that Calvin allowed for differing practices in the church and did not hold these instructions of Paul as binding on the church for all times and places, which is the issue with which the Christian Reformed Church is wrestling today. If John Calvin could allow the restrictive passages of 1 Corinthians 11 and 14, and by implication 1 Timothy 2, to be read on basically the grounds of seemliness and good order, then the proposed and questionable arguments for the timeless subordination of women are not a valid defense against women serving in the administrative offices of the church in the twentieth century. Nor is the bold allegation justified that charges proponents of women in office with employing a method of interpretation that undermines the authority and infallibility of the Scriptures. Such critics must then be prepared to include Calvin in their judgment of "liberal hermeneutics."

The church today is wrestling with a situation where the role of women has changed dramatically in society. It is a day in which there is an increased awareness of how women have been and continue to be the victims of pervasive discrimination and abuse. Calvin might well recognize that to expect women to be silent and defer to their husbands for instruction and prohibit them from teaching and occupying positions of authority under the conditions of our present situation does not work for seemliness and edification in the late twentieth century. Certainly in Christian churches today the limitation on women poses a hindrance to the furtherance of the gospel, which would be the paramount concern to the great missionary apostle. For Calvin, too, this is a basic consideration on which the church should decide such issues. We may recall his statement quoted above on 1 Corinthians 14:33–34 where he explicitly says, "For a situation can arise where there is need of such a kind as calls for a woman to speak." That time may have come.

Certainly in Christian churches today the limitation on women poses a hindrance to the furtherance of the gospel.

How, then, shall we account for the apostle's appeal to the Genesis data in 1 Timothy 2:13–14? We have observed that Paul's use of Genesis 2:18–24 is based upon the text as it was interpreted in his day. We have also noted that in 1 Corinthians 11:11–12 he suggested some ambivalence in his use of the text in the light of the New Testament teaching on "being in the Lord." As to his second argument, drawn from Genesis 3:1–7, 16, it was again evident that his application of the text reflected the contemporary understanding of Eve's role in the fall and its consequences for women. In view of the atoning work of Christ to undo the curse of the fall and the role of women in the resurrection event, however, the curse on Eve's sin appeared an unacceptable argument for disallowing women full equality in the church.

A reasonable explanation is that Paul adopts the reading and understanding of the Genesis material that was current in his day in order to effectively undergird his instructions to the Ephesian church. It is evident in 1 Timothy 2:7, as it is in 1 Corinthians, that Paul's authority as a teaching apostle was being questioned in Ephesus by the errant leaders. This accounts for the emphasis with which he states, "for this purpose I was appointed a herald and an apostle—I am telling the truth, I am not lying—and a teacher of the true faith to the Gentiles." He was therefore appealing, beyond his authority as an apostle, to God's word as they had received and interpreted it to support his restrictive instructions. It does not follow, however, that Paul's use of the Genesis data thereby endorses the quoted interpretation of the Genesis texts as divinely inspired truth to be universally applied in all circumstances and under all conditions. We have already seen the serious problems associated with the exposition of the Genesis texts as employed in 1 Timothy 2:14 were we to maintain their definitive authority in our times.

In support of this reading of Paul's use of the Genesis texts we call attention to a comment of Calvin on 1 Corinthians 14:36. He makes the interesting observation that "Paul does not use an argument with a universal bearing, but one that was especially applicable to the Corinthians, *something he is often in the habit of doing"* (Calvin's New Testament Commentaries, *Commentary on I Corinthians,* p. 307; emphasis added).

A pertinent example of this "habit" of Paul is found in 1 Corinthians 15:29, where he supports his teaching on the resurrection of the dead by arguing "Now if there is no resurrection, what will those do who are baptized for the dead? If the dead are not raised at all, why are people baptized for them?" Paul is obviously using an argument that has no weight for us. We cannot even be sure what is meant by his reference to baptism for the dead. But he uses it, we may assume, because it did have argumentative value for the people to whom he was writing.

All students of the Bible are aware of how New Testament authors quote the Old Testament to substantiate a point they are making, and that such use of quotations was an effective argument for their readers in that time. But such a practice is no longer valid in our use of scriptural quotations. This is not to say that the New Testament writers were wrong. We must always seriously seek to understand the validity of the teaching these authors are making through their quotations in order to know what the Word of God is saying to us in our times.

From this entire discussion on 1 Timothy 2 it is evident that the passage is not a clear, straightforward, compelling argument against women in office. The teaching of 1 Timothy 2:11–15 and 1 Corinthians 11:3–16 and 14:33–36, cannot be definitively quoted to restrict the momentous teaching of Galatians 3:28 on woman's equality in the Lord. First Timothy 2:11–15 is no Rock of Gibraltar. And Galatians 3:28 remains the Achilles' heel on which the case against women in office has no sure defense.

5

The Headship Principle
and Other Allegations

Several objections have been raised against permitting women to occupy the authoritative offices of teaching and administration in the church. In keeping with the purpose and focus of this book, my response to these allegations must be comparatively brief.

The Headship Principle

One issue that has entered the discussion on women in office in the Christian Reformed Church for more than fifteen years is the question of male headship over women. The question surfaced prominently in 1978 when Synod approved the ordination of qualified women to the office of deacon with the stipulation "provided that their work is distinguished from that of elders." This proviso was added out of a concern for the headship principle that holds that "the woman (wife) is to be subject to the man (husband)" (*Acts of Synod 1978,* p. 104). In 1979, in response to the wide- spread dissatisfaction with the 1978 decision on women deacons, Synod appointed its fourth study committee. Part of the task of this committee was "to study the implications of the ordination of women as deacons . . . giving specific attention to the concept of male headship and the nature of that authority" (*Acts of Synod 1979,* p. 122). The Synod of 1981 was not satisfied with the report of this committee and appointed yet another committee with the explicit task of examining the headship concept.

In 1984 Synod received the report from this "Committee on Headship in the Bible." The confusion that has troubled the church about the issue of headship became very appar- ent at Synod. In a ninety-four-page report the committee examined the biblical data relevant to the question of head- ship and presented Synod with a slim majority opinion of four out of seven members, which was later reduced to three when the reporter withdrew his support. The major- ity position held that the Scriptures teach the headship principle of men over women, not only in marriage and in the church, but also in all of society.

The committee's majority observed that the church had not provided clear biblical directives for structuring life according to the headship principle in society, and, as a consequence, Christians had followed "the prevailing winds of social and structural changes." The committee advised: "The church must speak to this issue. It is our conviction that the Scriptures teach the relevance of headship for the whole of life. The church must teach and proclaim it as such" (*Acts of Synod 1984,* p. 326).

The position of the majority was what had been the Chris- tian church's consistent position on the relation of men and women, grounded on what was believed to be the creation order. The Medieval Schoolmen, including Thomas Aquinas, on the basis of Genesis 2 and 3, considered woman an inferior variety of humankind. The Reformers, too, were emphatic in maintaining women's subjection to men in all things. Martin Luther held there was no divine warrant for a woman to occupy a ruling position. He maintained that even a woman serving as a queen in the place of a king did not confirm the rule of woman. John Calvin had a somewhat higher view of woman's role and ability, but in commenting on 1 Timothy 2:12 he writes that women are born to obey, adding "all wise men have always rejected . . . the government of women, as a natural monstrosity" (Calvin's New Testament Commentaries, *Commentary on I Timothy,* p. 217). John Knox, in his feud with Mary, Queen of Scots, applied his Calvinistic training about women's place with the proposition: "To promote a woman to bear rule, superiority, dominion or empire above any nation, realm or city, is repugnant to nature; contumely to God, a thing most contrarious to his revealed will and approved ordinance; and finally it is the subversion of good order, of all equity and justice" (quoted by Paul K. Jewett in *Man as Male and Female,* p. 68).

Western civilization has long practiced male dominance over women and found support in the Judeo-Christian teaching on women's subordination rooted in the supposed creation ordinance. It must be remembered that woman suffrage in the United States has only existed for some seventy years, and at the time it was enacted, many in the church opposed giving women the right to vote and hold office in government. But in 1984 the committee's majority was right in pointing out that "the prevailing winds of social and structural change" had restrained the church from speaking out against the growing equality of women in society.

---

*Thus the church quietly laid
aside what had been for nearly
two millennia the unquestioned
status of man's priority and dominance in society on the basis of
the creation order.*

The position of the majority met with no support at Synod and was tabled (dismissed). Later Synod declared "there is insufficient scriptural evidence to warrant the conclusion that a headship principle . . . is a creation norm extending over the whole of human life" (*Acts of Synod 1984*, p. 624). No negative votes were recorded. Thus the church quietly laid aside what had been for nearly two millennia the unquestioned status of man's priority and dominance in society on the basis of the creation order.

It is revealing that the challenge with which the committee's majority of 1984 confronted the church has been almost completely ignored and lost in the debate. They threw down the gauntlet to either affirm the headship principle of men over women in all of society, or to acknowledge the inconsistency of employing a double standard and being guilty of an obvious injustice in restricting women from holding office in the church. This is what they said: "To teach that women may hold any position open to them in such areas as business, education, and government but that when it comes to the life of the church they may not hold ecclesiastical office indeed appears to be a double-standard. . . . *To deny them such positions in the life of the instituted church has correctly been perceived by many as inconsistent and unjust"* (*Acts of Synod 1984,* pp. 324–26; emphasis added). Synod declared that as yet there is "insufficient scriptural evidence" for the right of women to hold office in the church.

The following year the advisory committee of the Synod of 1985 acknowledged that the 1984 committee had "built a strong case for extending 'headship' of all men over all women from marriage to the church and to all of society" but that Synod had "refused to recognize that the headship of males over females extended to society in general." There has been a significant silence among opponents of women in office to explain why the headship principle rooted in the creation order is not applicable to "all of society." It appears to be an embarrassment that the opponents prefer to ignore, in the light "of the woman's changing role and place" in modern society. If any reference is made to the issue, it is usually passed over with some bland remark that the limitation on woman's authority does not appear biblically to extend to male/female relationships in society. It is also telling that opponents have avoided discussing the difficult question how the authority of a husband is to be exercised in the family if his authority over his wife does not extend beyond the home into society.

There has been a significant silence among opponents of women in office to explain why the headship principle rooted in the creation order is not applicable to "all of society."

One of the two minority opinions submitted in 1984 picked up the gauntlet and judged "there is not sufficiently clear evidence from Scripture to warrant the conclusion of a 'headship principle', holding that man's rulership over woman is a creation norm" (*Acts of Synod 1984,* p. 376). This report called into question whether the Scriptures teach male headship in society, church, or marriage on the basis of the creation order. Synod rejected this minority position, declaring that "the headship principle, which means that the man should exercise primary leadership and direction-setting in the home and in the church, is a biblical teaching recognized in both the Old and New Testament" (*Acts of Synod 1984,* p. 623).

> *The headship principle provides no scriptural warrant for barring women from office in the church.*

It was inevitable that the question should persist. If the headship of man does not extend to all of society, why does the headship of man apply to the church? Thus in 1987 Synod appointed yet another committee to provide clear biblical and confessional grounds for extending the principle of headship from marriage to the church. This "Committee to Study Headship" reported in 1990 that weighty arguments could be raised both for and against the issue of headship as it bore on the question of women in church office. It made no recommendations on the issue, but advised Synod to encourage churches to continue "critical reflection and discussion."

It was when this inconclusive report was on the floor of the Synod of 1990 that the delegates decided by a margin of fifteen votes to cut the Gordian knot and "permit churches to use their discretion in utilizing the gifts of women members in all the offices of the church" (*Acts of Synod of 1990,* p. 650). Synod stated that the report of the study committee on headship "taken as a whole, does not 'provide clear biblical and confessional grounds for extending the 'headship principle' from marriage to the church'" (*Acts of Synod 1990,* p. 654). In 1992 the ad hoc committee formulated this declaration of Synod as its third ground in support of the 1990 Synod's decision stating, "The scriptural teaching that the husband is head over his wife within marriage cannot be broadened to claim the headship of all males over all females in the church and so to prohibit women from serving in the offices of the church" (*Agenda of Synod 1992,* p. 377).

The question whether the so-called headship principle in marriage must be extended to the church remains a pertinent issue in the debate. The biblical passages that opponents cite in defense of extending the headship principle in the church, thereby restricting women from serving as elders and ministers, consist principally of Genesis 2:18–24; 1 Corinthians 11:3–16; 14:33–36; and 1 Timothy 2:11–15. These passages we have discussed in the previous chapter and found unconvincing. The headship principle provides no scriptural warrant for barring women from office in the church.

That there is an ineradicable distinction of sex between men and women is obvious. This difference is precisely what makes the fellowship and partnership in marriage not only possible but mutually fulfilling. But to extend the idea of headship from marriage to the church, apart from it being without scriptural warrant, raises many knotty questions on which opponents of women in office are by no means agreed in their answers. Does headship apply only to the submission of wives to their husbands in the life of the church as in 1 Corinthians 14:34–35? If so, why are single women and widows barred from serving in the authoritative offices? Why is it maintained that wives may not exercise authority over their husbands in occupying the offices of elder or minister, but they may do so in society? Should not the church on the basis of headship restrict wives who are members of the church from holding positions in society in which they may exercise authority over their husbands? Is not the 1984 majority committee report correct in pointing out the inconsistency of applying a double standard that amounts to injustice to women (*Acts of Synod 1984,* p. 324)?

May we not conclude that a woman's submission in the sphere of the home does not preclude her leadership in the sphere of the church, as all appear agreed that it does not preclude her leadership in society?

What significance in this context should be attached to the Reformed concept of sphere sovereignty as it impinges on the husband/wife relationship in society and the church? John Calvin pointed out, in commenting on 1 Timothy 2:12, "that there is no absurdity in a man's commanding and obeying at the same time in different relationships" (Calvin's New Testament Commentaries, *Commentary on I Timothy,* p. 217). Calvin, of course, did not apply this to women, but is it not a relevant consideration in our day? May we not conclude that a woman's submission in the sphere of the home does not preclude her leadership in the sphere of the church, as all appear agreed that it does not preclude her leadership in society?

In the light of our conclusion that the Old and New Testaments do not restrict women for all times and places from occupying the authoritative offices in the church, and in the face of so much uncertainty among opponents of women in office regarding the application of the headship principle, it is apparent that a woman's role in the church cannot be definitively prohibited on the ground of the purported headship principle. The fact is that although the house of male headship stood for centuries, the twentieth-century winds of change have blown it down. It has proved to be built upon the sand of an indefensible reading of the Bible.

> *Although the house of male headship stood for centuries, the twentieth-century winds of change have blown it down.*

How the equality and partnership of men and women as image-bearers of God taught in Genesis and their renewed equality in Christ as declared in Galatians 3:28 are to be related to the concept of male headship in marriage as found in Ephesians 5:21–33; Colossians 3:24; and 1 Peter 3:1–6, is beyond the scope of this book. The ad hoc committee, in keeping with the generally accepted position of the study committees, assumed in its report that "the Bible clearly teaches the headship of the husband in marriage" (*Agenda of Synod 1992,* p. 377). But what constitutes male headship in marriage will no doubt continue to be a matter of study and debate in the church.

Egalitarianism and Homosexuality

On the floor of the Synod of 1992 a delegate leveled a serious attack against the ad hoc committee's report. He charged that behind the report lurked a modern philosophical egalitarianism that advocates the absolute equality of all people in worth, function, and authority in all spheres of life. Egalitarianism, he said, is the evil deification and absolutizing of the otherwise good idea of "equality," one that opposes all levels of authority and obedience, maintaining there is no superiority or subordination in society. It is a humanistically inspired liberation movement that is in rebellion against God's creation order. He found its appearance in the ad hoc committee's report. But the report is quasi-egalitarian, he alleged, because it did not go the whole way and deny male superordination in marriage.

He granted that Scripture is, in some measure, egalitarian in teaching an equality of worth and gifts to men and women, and an equality of authority in their exercise of the cultural mandate. He even conceded that the Bible seemed to allow for women's authority to extend to male/female relationships in society. But, he maintained, the ad hoc committee crossed the line into egalitarianism when it affirmed the equality of authority for men and women in the church.

In the critic's judgment, the committee evidenced its egalitarianism by its appeal to an alleged unwarranted interpretation of Galatians 3:28. From his perspective "the linchpin of the whole argument . . . for women in authoritative offices is a rather imaginative . . . inconsistently applied interpretation of Galatians 3:28 based on egalitarianism." The committee, he charged, had "to engage in exegetical gymnastics or hermeneutical leap-frogging to make Galatians 3:28 into the emancipation and proclamation verse of the Bible." He also criticized the committee's reading of 1 Timothy 2:11–12 in which, he was confident, "the relationship of male headship to women in the church did receive divine grounding in Paul's appeal to the order of creation and of the fall." The reader can judge whether the exegesis of Galatians 3:28 in chapter 3 and the interpretation of 1 Timothy 2:11–15 in chapter 5 are not a sufficient reply to the critic's allegations regarding the use of these texts. The entire basis for the speaker's criticism rested on his interpretation of Galatians 3:28 and 1 Timothy 2:11–12.

What the delegate did not consider was that the equality taught in Galatians 3:28, and espoused by the ad hoc committee, does not reject all hierarchy as does radical egalitarianism. Society, the church, and the family would all sink into anarchy if humankind were to live by a pure egalitarian model. Of course, there must be levels of authority and obedience, of authorities and subordinates in all areas of society as Scripture also teaches. What Galatians 3:28 teaches, as we explained in chapter 3, is that in Christ gender is no barrier to potential for worth, function, responsibility, and authority in the church, any more than ethnic or social distinctions. Such equality does not mean that all men and all women are equally competent and qualified to exercise authority in the church; neither *all* men nor *all* women are gifted to serve as elders and ministers. The point of Galatians 3:28 is that their qualifications are not limited by ethnicity, social status, or gender.

Such equality does not mean that all men and all women are equally competent and qualified to exercise authority in the church.

A comparison with the Declaration of Independence and the Constitution of the United States of America will illustrate the point. The former document declares "that all men are created equal, that they are endowed by their Creator with certain unalienable Rights . . . that to secure these rights, Governments are instituted . . . deriving their just powers from the consent of the governed." The equality of all citizens before the government and its laws does not mean, however, that all citizens hold office or are qualified to hold office. The Constitution contains numerous qualifications that citizens must meet to be in office. Since the enactment of the Nineteenth Amendment gender is no longer among the qualifications and both men and women are eligible to be elected or appointed to office. So, in Christ, a Christian's gender is no limitation to his or her role in the church. The lack of various qualifications may limit a person's access to an ecclesiastical office, such as physical handicap, mental retardation, emotional instability, lack of necessary education, or family or other limiting obligations, but a person's gender is not among them.

In the delegate's judgment, it was a puzzling inconsistency that the ad hoc committee should have given Galatians 3:28 priority over 1 Timothy 2:11–12, but not allow it to have priority, for example, over Ephesians 5:22–33, and thereby dispense with male headship in marriage. We have noted above that the mandate of the ad hoc committee was specifically not to be the seventh study committee, but its task was to "gather from the various synodical study-committee reports and related publications the biblical grounds" for the 1990 Synod's decision to open all ecclesiastical offices to women. The ad hoc committee therefore did not go outside of its mandate to question the teaching of male headship in the family; it assumed such headship as the synodical study committee reports did.

That the New Testament teaching on the equality of women in Christ has implications for the relationship between husbands and wives is plainly discernible in Ephesians 5:22–33. The relation of a husband to his wife as described in this passage is a far cry from the harsh curse in Genesis 3:16 that decreed he would rule over his wife. The marriage relationship is not the relationship of a military commander giving orders to a soldier, or a master ordering a slave, or parents requiring obedience of their children. Contrary to the older marriage forms, the Bible nowhere orders a wife to "obey" her husband, but it does enjoin her to respect and to be in submission to him, as the Scriptures also teach we are to be in submission to each other out of reverence for Christ (Eph. 5:21). The love between husband and wife is as intimate as the love of Christ for his church, and a man's love for his own body. Submission is not simply another word for obedience in the New Testament, although it may include obedience. Submission has to do with readiness to renounce one's own will for the sake of others (*Theological Dictionary of the New Testament,* 8:41–45). Precisely what all this implies and to what extent calls into question the headship principle in marriage were matters beyond the scope of the ad hoc committee's mandate and are outside the purpose of this book. Genesis 2:18–25 and Ephesians 5:22–33, in my judgment, fit the model of a husband/wife partnership in marriage far better than the hierarchical structure of the man's superiority and the woman's subservience within marriage.

Submission has to do with readiness to renounce one's own will for the sake of others.

The speaker argued that since the ad hoc committee's exegesis of Galatians 3:28 and 1 Timothy 2:11–12 allowed women to serve in the ecclesiastical offices, the committee, using proper logic, should have denied male headship in marriage. But that conclusion the committee did not make because it asserted "the Bible clearly teaches the headship of the husband in marriage." Therefore, the delegate maintained, the committee's exegesis of the Galatians and Timothy texts was obviously wrong. The argument, in my judgment, can be equally well reversed. If the interpretation of the Galatians and Timothy passages in this treatise is correct, then the result may mean that we need to reread Ephesians 5:22–33 concerning headship in marriage.

The delegate particularly aroused the apprehension of the others when he proceeded to allege that the committee's use of Galatians 3:28 could lead to the ordination of practicing homosexuals. By what principle of interpretation would the church be prevented from ordaining practicing gays into the ministry, he asked (by repeatedly referring to "practicing" gays, he appeared to allow for celibate homosexuals to be ordained).

By what principle of interpretation would practicing homosexuals be barred from ordination? By the same principle by which adulterers and fornicators are barred from ordination. As long as the church understands that the Bible teaches that homosexual practice is sin, practicing gays are disqualified for office.

The charge is made by opponents that the method that proponents of women in office use to interpret the Bible can equally well be used to condone homosexual behavior. The allegation is not true. We have seen in chapter 2 that the issue of women's ordination arises out of two strains of thought in the New Testament: women's equality in Christ and passages that seem to restrict their authority in the ruling and teaching offices. The entire debate concerning women in office arises out of the paradox of these two lines of teaching in the Bible that must be reconciled in order that we may know how to guide the church in its use of women's gifts. The biblical teaching on homosexual practice poses no such paradox; it is consistently opposed to homosexual practice. The speaker's interjection of homosexuality into the discussion on the floor of Synod created unfortunate confusion.

First Timothy 3:1–12 on Ordination

Those who are opposed to women serving as ministers and elders often cite Paul's instructions on the qualifications for officebearers in 1 Timothy 3:1–12 as explicitly teaching that an elder is to be "the husband of one wife" and that a deacon "must be the husband of but one wife." They conclude from this passage, along with the identical clause in Titus 1:6, that women are thus excluded from the ruling offices of the congregation. But it is evident that the purpose of including the clause "husband of one wife" is not to make sure that the overseer be a male, but that he not be a polygamist.

But if it be argued that the clause implicitly restricts the office to males, anyone who has come this far in reading this book knows the answer to this argument. The same concerns in the church in Ephesus, which occasioned Paul's restraints on women in the worship services (1 Tim. 2:11–14) for the well-being of the church and the further-ance of the gospel as we learned in chapter 5, account for the apostle's directives in this text. It may be pointed out that should anyone insist on reading the passage in a very strict, literal way, it would require of him or her to hold that only married elders and deacons who have children are eli-gible for office. In the setting that occasioned the writing of Paul's letter to Timothy, and in view of the injunctions in 1 Timothy 2:11–12, which immediately precede the listing of qualifications for officebearers in chapter 3, the apostle's exclusion of women is what would be expected. But it would also be expected that the gender qualification is not to be interpreted as a universal, timeless prohibition against women serving as elders and ministers, any more than is true of 1 Timothy 2:11–12.

A Crisis in Interpreting the Bible?

Some critics, who are strenuously opposed to women in office, avow that "there can be no doubt that the Christian Reformed denomination is fighting for its life over the issue of women in office. Many church members are convinced that the difference of opinion over women's ordination is due to differing views of Scriptural authority and hermeneu-tics (the method of interpreting Scripture). Indeed, many are convinced that the very doctrinal foundation of the church is in jeopardy." The differing hermeneutics, it is alleged, "pits the alleged Scriptural principle of the equality and correlativity of men and women against the specific teaching of those Scriptural texts which describe a differentiation of roles" (Nelson D. Kloosterman and Cornelius P. Venema, *A Cause for Division: The Hermeneutic of Women's Ordination,* pp. 5–6). The references are clearly to the biblical interpretations proponents of women in office have advanced in synodical study committee reports and elsewhere. The authors are alarmed by Dr. John W. Cooper's *A Cause for Division? Women in Office and the Unity of the Church,* in which, they charge, he "defends the argument for women's ordination with a hermeneutic which is at odds with our historic position as Reformed believers." They also maintain that his hermeneutic not only "provide[s] no Scriptural proof for its notion of equality between men and women, but it also discounts those texts which spell out God's blessed order for the relationships between men and women in the home and church" (p. 6).

Contrary to what is so radically alleged by these opponents, an interpretation of the scriptural data supporting women in office is possible without calling into question our Reformed confession of the Scriptures as the divinely inspired and infallible Word of God. This book is devoted to a study of the relevant passages and cannot be dismissed by the readers as employing an un-Reformed method of interpretation. Quite the contrary, the method of interpretation has followed the doctrine of Scripture and the principles of Reformed hermeneutics as taught by my teacher, Professor Louis Berkhof. This method involves a careful study of the words of the text to determine its meaning, the literary context of the text, and the historical factors that influenced its composition. A crucially important element of the method includes determining the message of the text in the whole of the Scriptures that constitutes an organic unity and forms the text's analogical framework. Critics may be able to fault the accuracy and conclusions arrived at in this book, but they cannot base their critique on the employment of an un-Reformed hermeneutic.

Changes in the world have always required the church to restudy the Bible to interpret it in new and fresh ways.

It is true that those who favor opening all the offices of the church to qualified women have been challenged, in the light of the changing role of women in society, to reread Scripture in order to learn what it teaches, and possibly to understand it in ways that did not occur to them before. Changes in the world have always required the church to restudy the Bible to interpret it in new and fresh ways. It was true for the church in Galileo's day when astronomy taught it was the sun that was the center of the solar system and not the earth. It was true during the abolition of slavery in the nineteenth century that passages regarding slavery had to be reinterpreted. In our own day, Reformed Christians in South Africa have had to revise their interpretation of Scripture as justifying apartheid. The Synod of 1984, in the presence of widespread acceptance of equality for women in the marketplace and society at large, was forced to reread the centuries-old understanding of the biblical data on male dominance in all of society.

Neither the Synod of 1984, nor those of us who are committed to permitting women to serve in the ecclesiastical offices of the Christian Reformed Church, call into question the authority and infallibility of the Scriptures as we study the Bible anew to understand its teaching on the status of women in the church. Changes in society require us to search the Scriptures in the light of the questions that such changes raise, but it must be clearly understood that the changes do not determine the way in which the Scriptures shall be interpreted. From the Reformed perspective the Scriptures themselves are the final authority for their own interpretation.

We have long known the slogan "to be Reformed is always to be reforming." It is not only permissible but ever required of us to understand and explain the Scriptures so they may be God's Word for us in our day, but it is not permissible for us to question the authority of the Bible in matters of faith and practice, by evaluating, judging, or criticizing the Bible with extrabiblical data and criteria.

To refuse to reread the Bible and be open to new insights and understandings, is to be unfaithful to the Scriptures as the living Word of God and to resist the Holy Spirit whom Jesus promised will lead us into all the truth. The perennial directive of Paul to Timothy is apropos: "Study to shew thyself approved unto God, a workman that needeth not to be ashamed, rightly dividing the word of truth" (2 Tim. 2:15 AV).

Conclusion: *A Pastoral Concern*

My purpose in writing this book was to help members of the Christian Reformed Church read the Bible in such a way that allows for and even approves of ordaining women as ministers and elders in the congregations. Not all readers may be convinced that this interpretation is right, but they cannot say it calls into question the divine inspiration and infallibility of the Scriptures.

It is our task to seek in all honesty to "correctly handle the word of truth" (2 Tim. 2:15), lest we willfully abuse the Scriptures. There was a time in history when slavery was a moral advance in human society. Instead of an enemy being deprived of life by death, he was allowed to live in bondage to his conqueror. The Scriptures were written in that period of history, and the gospel addresses the moral dimensions of that situation for both masters and slaves. But it also so undermined the institution that in the course of history it became immoral to continue the support of slavery. Today we know it was no minor fault for nineteenth-century Christians to misread the Scriptures to defend the institution of slavery that inflicted so much human suffering and abuse. In our own times, we have witnessed the tragic results of Reformed believers misreading the Bible in South Africa to support apartheid with all the injustices and misery it has caused and continues to cause.

In a world where physical strength was important to protect and provide for a family, and the woman was restricted by her maternal and familial roles, it was natural that the man should take leadership and primary responsibility and that the woman should be dependent upon the man. In a sinful world it was also true that such male primacy would lead to repression and demeaning dominance over the woman. The Bible was written in the society of male supremacy and female subordination. As the Word of God for that time it addressed the moral dimensions of that culture with an ameliorating influence that distinguished the position of women among the Jews from the peoples around them. The New Testament marked an even greater advance in woman's position and role, and infused the church with the sense of male and female equality in the Lord. Now the Christian church in the latter half of the twentieth century has become aware of the discrimination and injustice that society has imposed on women throughout history. All of us now recognize the right of women to equality in society. We no longer quote the Bible to promote the subordination and discrimination of women in society at large.

The issue we face is whether we must continue to prohibit women from serving the church with their gifts as elders and ministers. *It is no minor matter.* On the one hand, to disregard the supposedly clear teaching of Scripture in order to allow for the ordination of women would be to violate the authority of the Bible. On the other, to continue to limit "the privileges of full communion" of the women of the church, unless plainly restricted by the Word of God, is morally unjust.

There is no consensus among us on what the Scriptures teach concerning women in office. In this dilemma the

Synod of 1990 decided to permit each congregation to use its discretion in utilizing the gifts of women in all the offices of the church. The response to the decision has resulted in a severe crisis in the church. In this difficult time for the Christian Reformed Church, our witness to the furtherance of the gospel in the world is being discredited and the well-being of our fellowship has been seriously harmed. These consequences would be of prime concern for the apostle Paul and must be for us.

> *To continue to limit "the privileges of full communion" of the women of the church, unless plainly restricted by the Word of God, is morally unjust.*

The controversy centers on the question: What do the Scriptures teach on the issue of women in office? It is my prayer that this book will contribute to our continuing discussion as we seek to answer that question and live accordingly.